HOSTINGS: OCULAR LAB, 2003–10

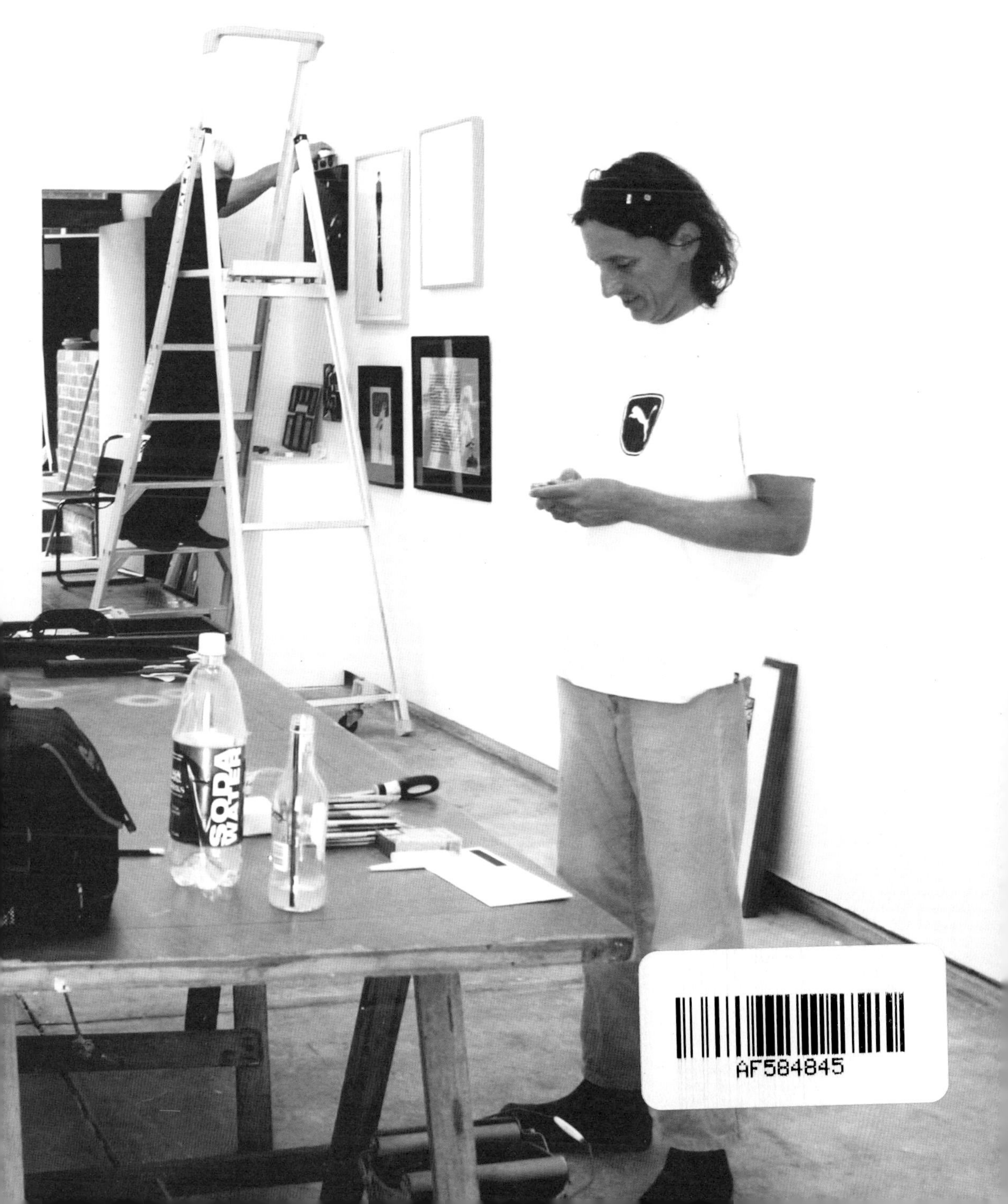

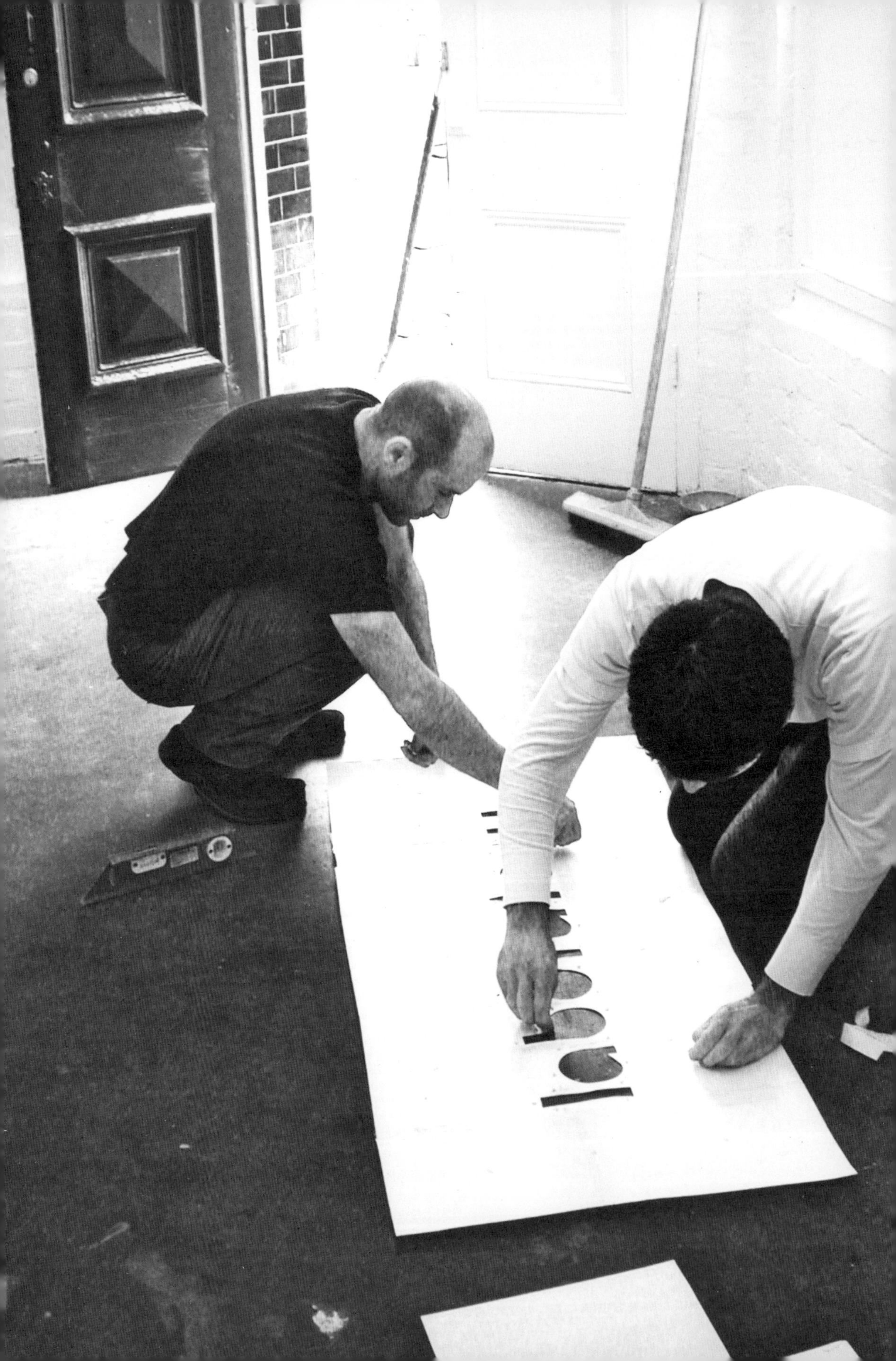

HOSTINGS:
OCULAR LAB, 2003–10

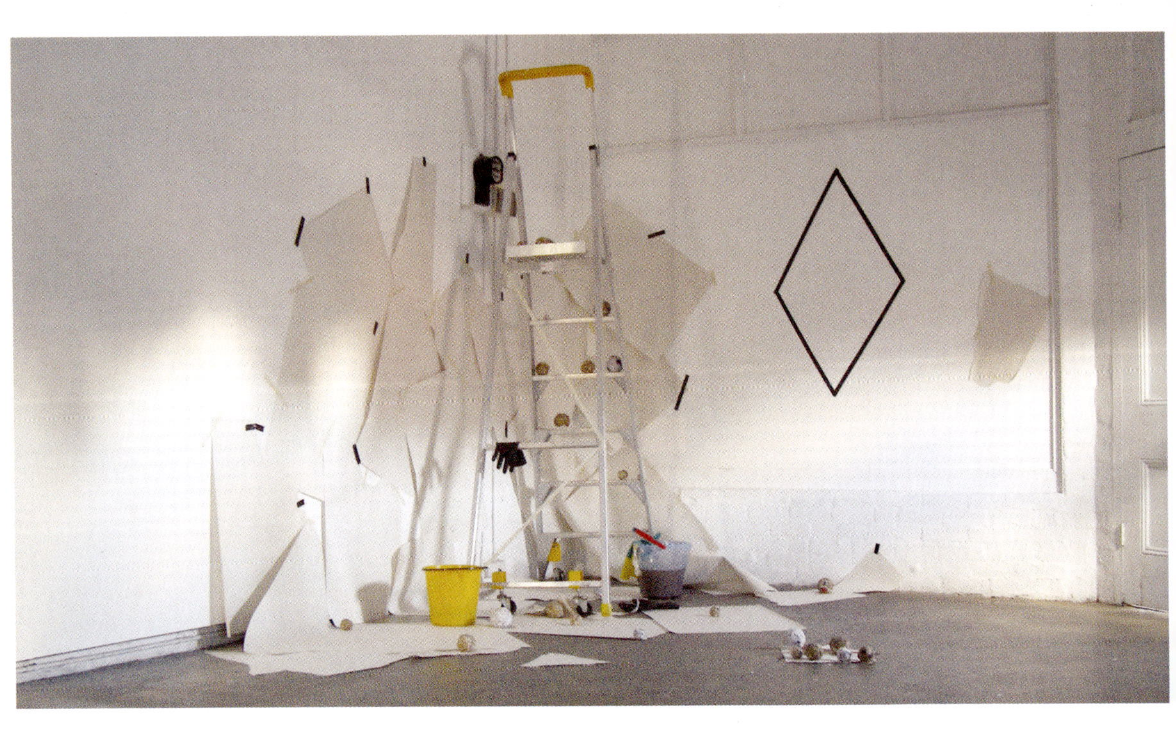

Mia Salsjo
Evolving installation during a one-month residency
performance installation as a closing event
2007

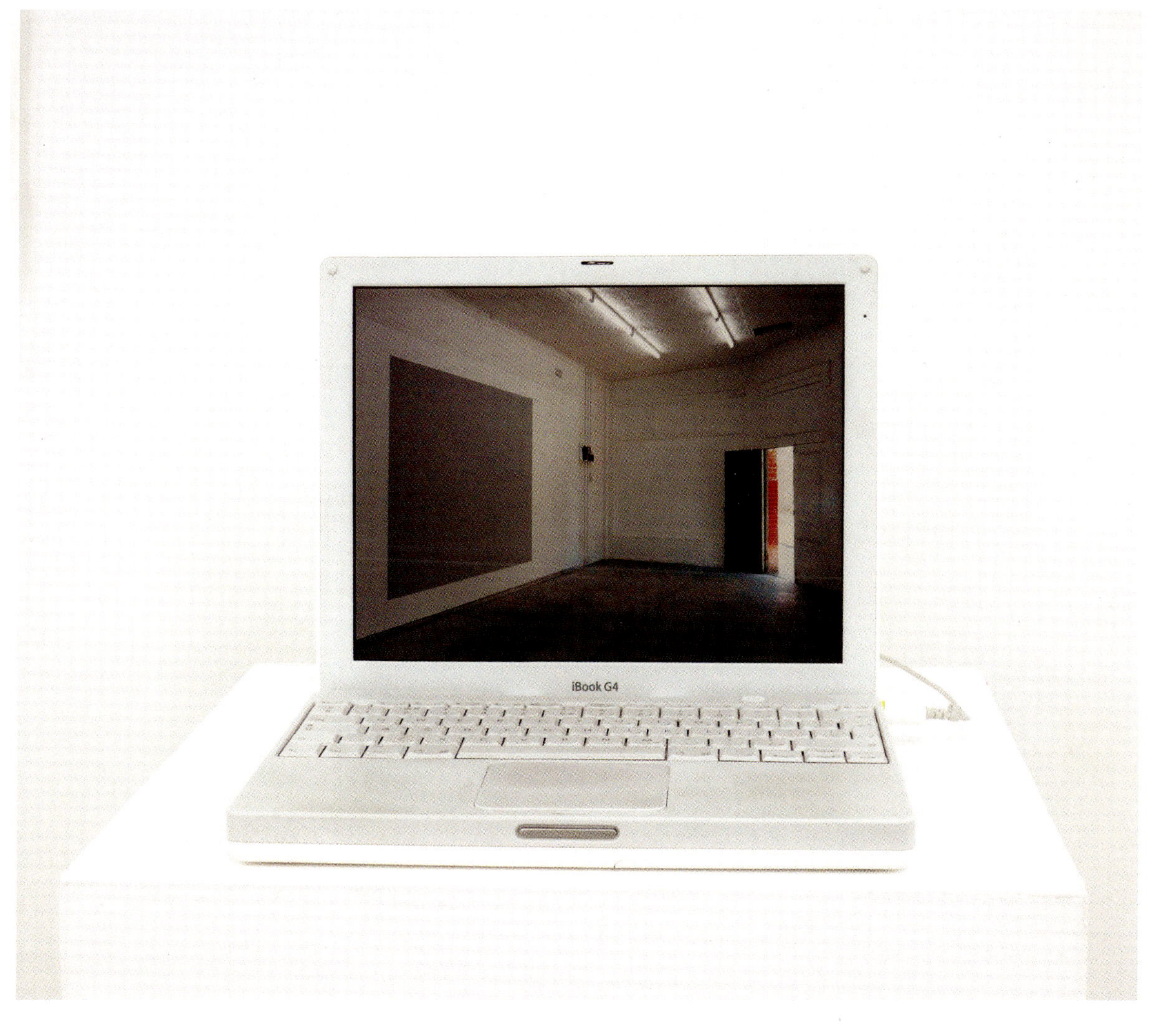

Ian Whittlesea (UK)
A SLOW FADE. TO BLACK
time-based installation, wall painting, acrylic on wood
2008

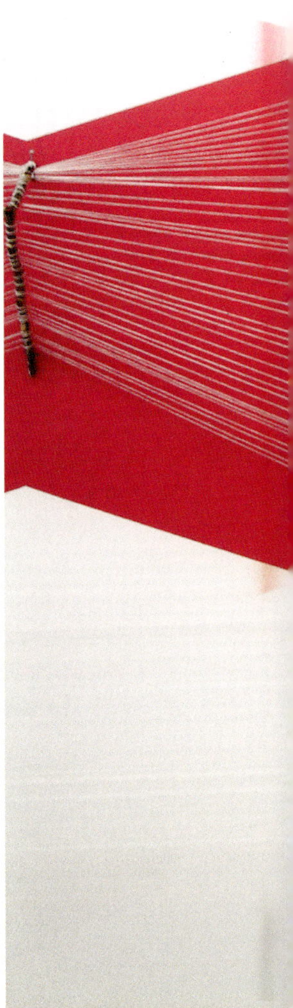

Melanie Irwin
Architectonic Traces
installation: acrylic paint, string, sticks
2008

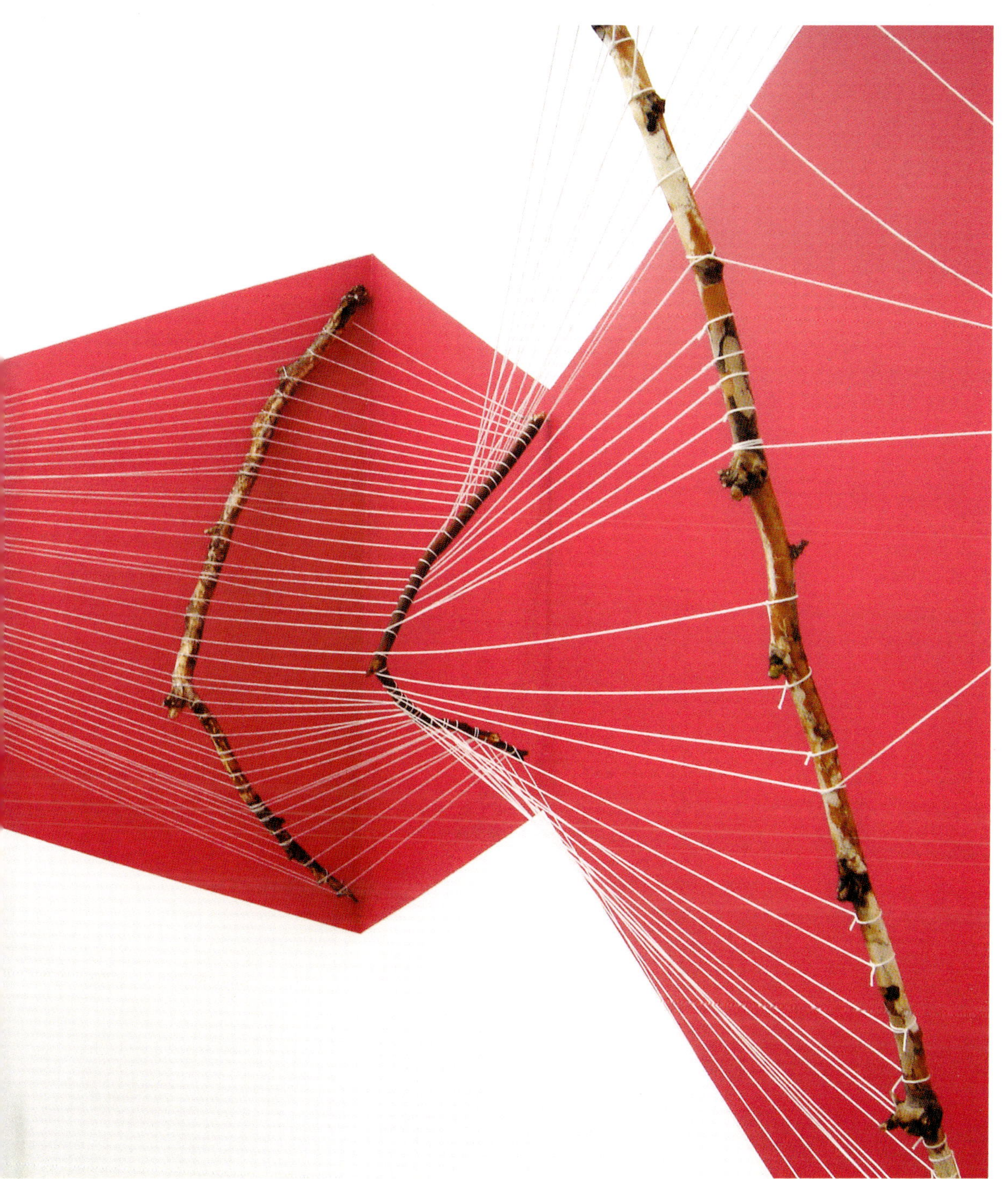

Greg Richards
Autopilot
high density polystyrene, vinyl contact
2005
photograph: Greg Richards

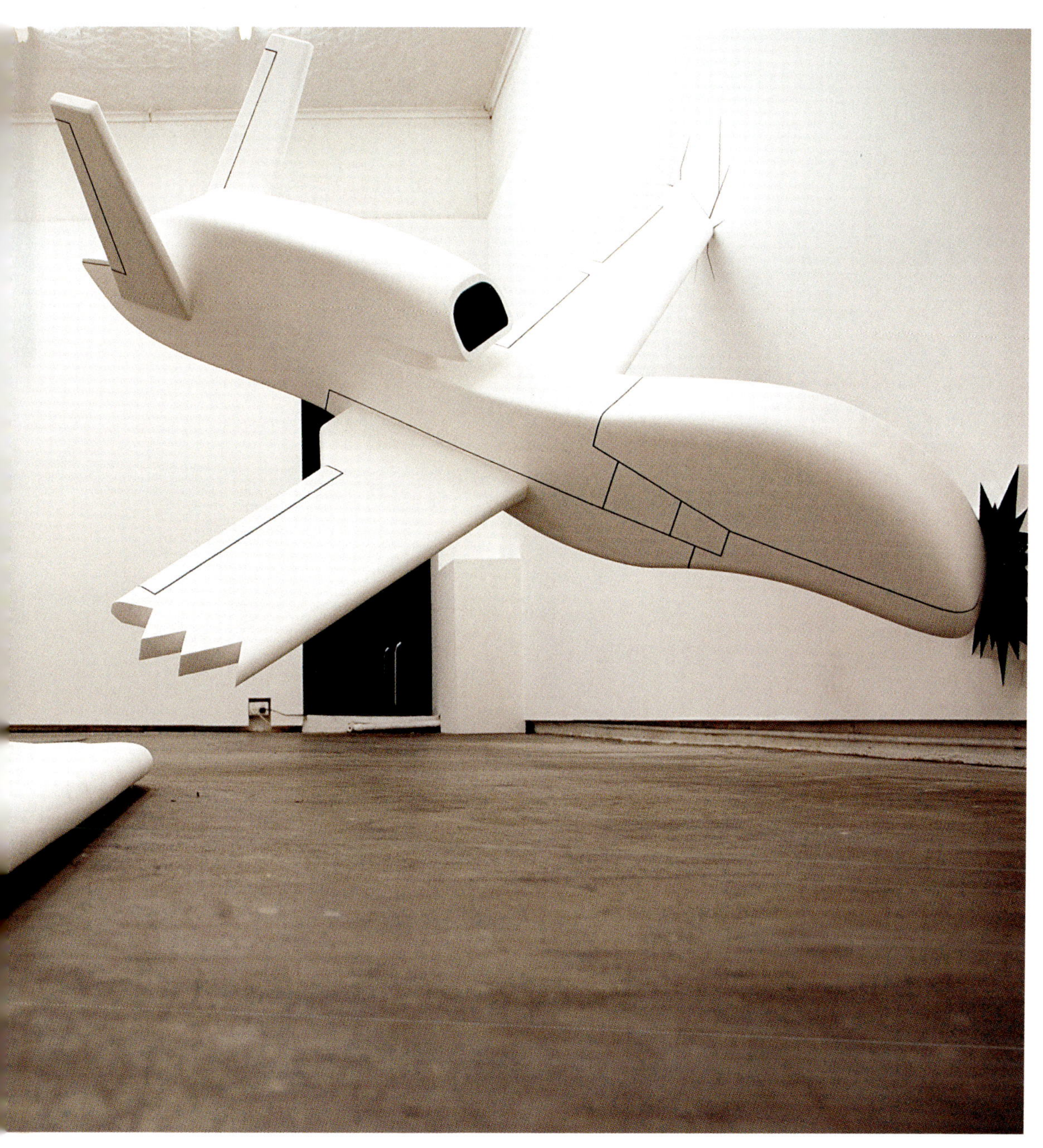

The Doppler Effect #2 The Question Archive Melbourne

Kelly Large and Ruth Claxton 2005

79. I was just wondering what one would think of the opening scene of the film Blue Velvet by David Lynch? Should I describe it? Well if you have seen the film it's the opening scene where the aah camera pans round under the ground, that's probably enough information for you, see the film.

80. How do you escape your own aesthetic?

81. Um, umm, I am wondering whether or not you, you think Australia should be a republic?

82. What is punk?

83. How long can I rob Peter to pay Paul?

84. What happened to the man, er, who was dying of cancer that I met er at the Greek Orthodox monastery in Essex?

85. Er, do the presence of creeks or rivers in your neighbourhood inspire you at all?

86. Um, what do people do all day?

87. Why is everything so purple?

opposite:
Ruth Claxton (UK) and Kelly Large (UK)
Doppler Effect #2
The Question Archive
A5 publication: cover
2005

above:
Ruth Claxton (UK) and Kelly Large (UK)
Doppler Effect #2
The Question Archive
A5 publication: text
2005

Richard Lewer
drawing – from studio to situation
with Vin Ryan and John Abbate
performance/installation, black acrylic wall text, sound
2005
courtesy the artist and Fehily Contemporary

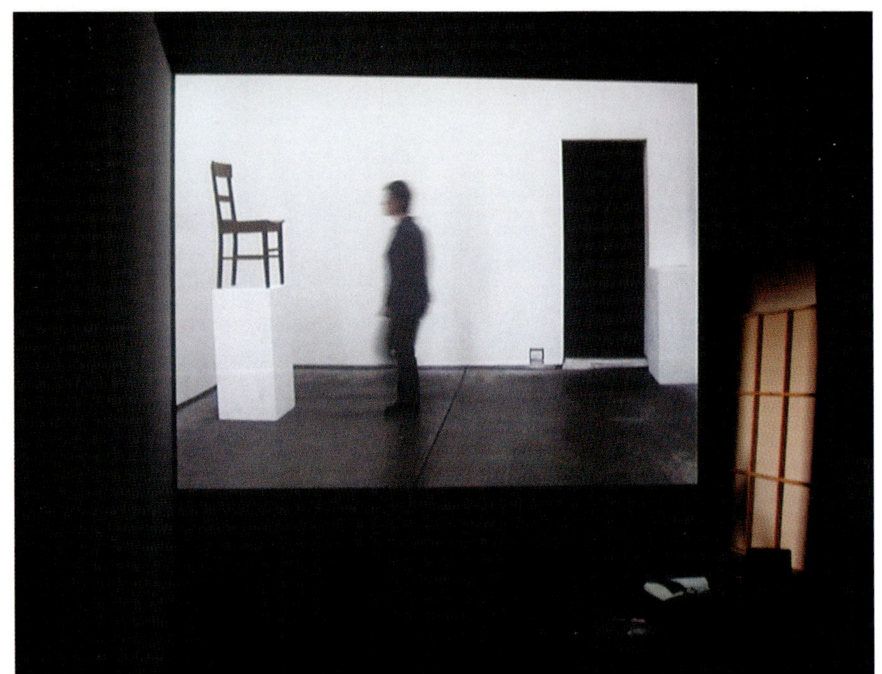

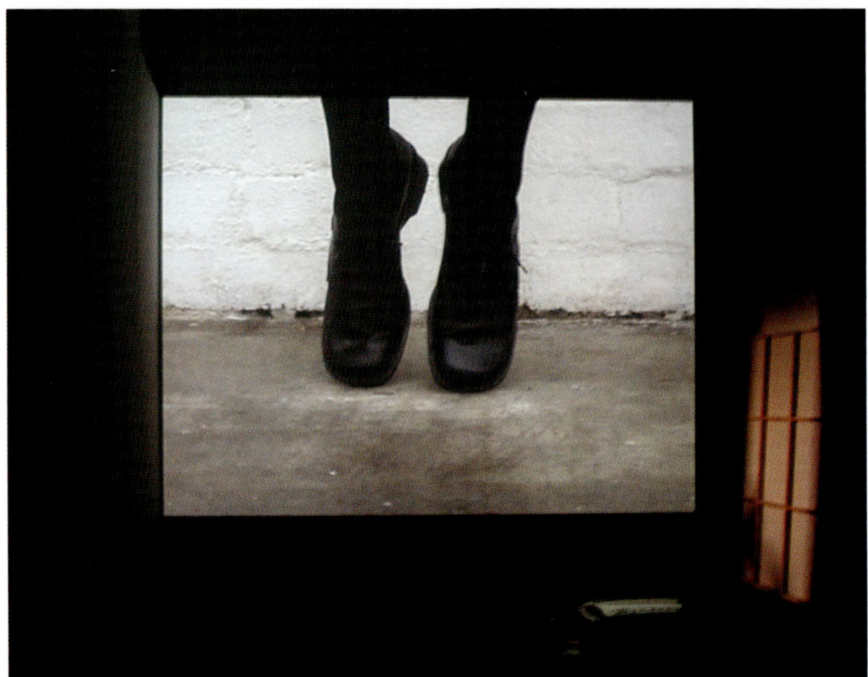

Sandra Bridie and Cynthia Troup
Wait
video project
2004

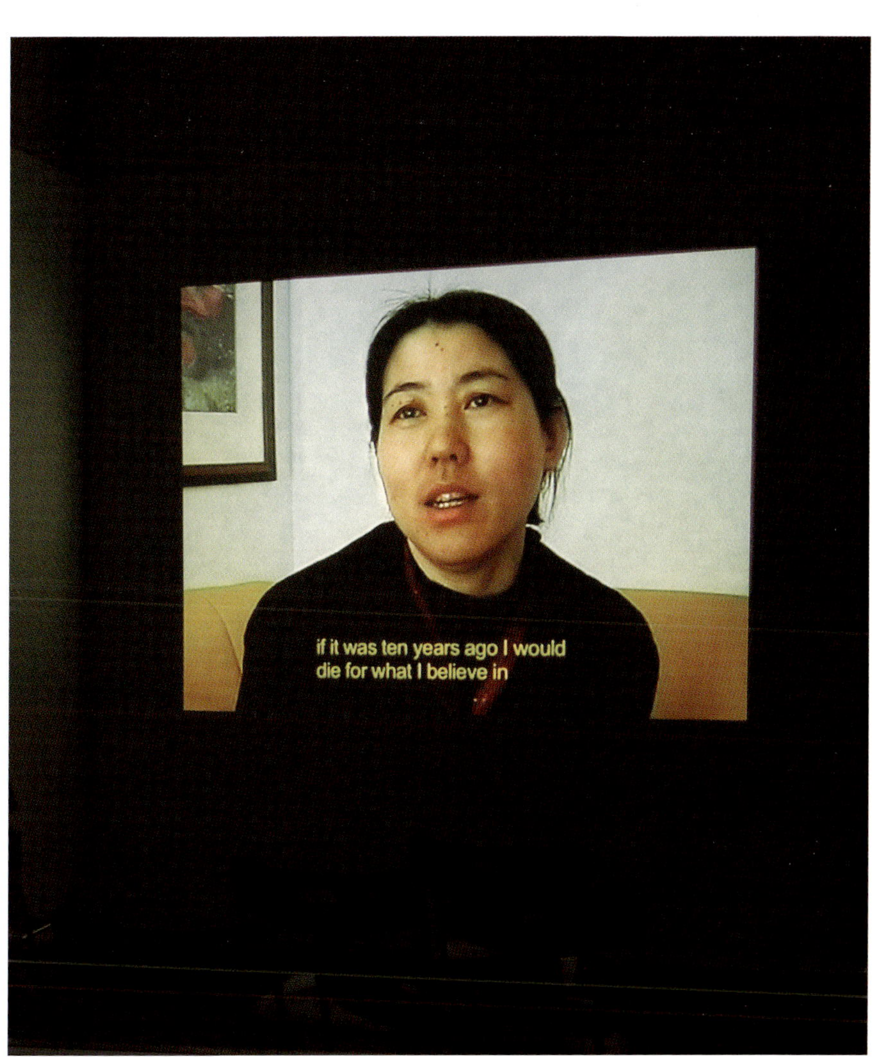

Kylie Wilkinson
NATIONALISM: What are you talking about?
video projection
2006

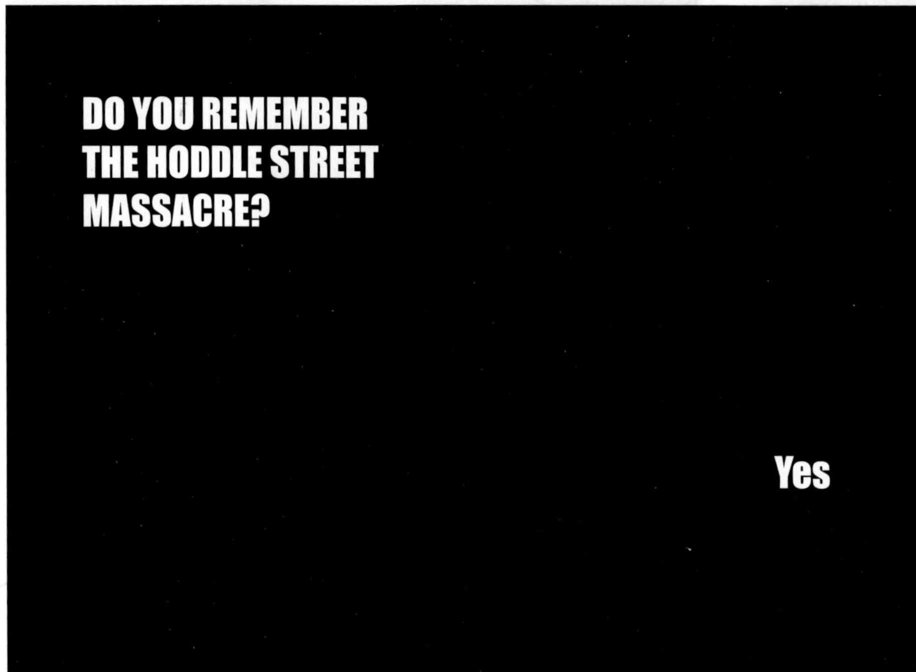

Elvis Richardson
The Hoddle Street Massacre
DVD with sound
2005
courtesy the artist and Hugo Michell Gallery

opposite top:
Julie Davies and Sandra Bridie
Julie Davies, Composite Portraits of Sandra Bridie
S.B. walking past an image of the installation of Andrew Hurle: One Place: Tokyo 1995
digital print
2007/2008
courtesy the artists and Place Gallery

opposite bottom:
Julie Davies and Sandra Bridie
Julie Davies, Composite Portraits of Sandra Bridie
Documentation of cataloguing the Robert Schubert Collection for the Ocular Lab library is projected onto S.B.
digital print
2007/2008
courtesy the artists and Place Gallery

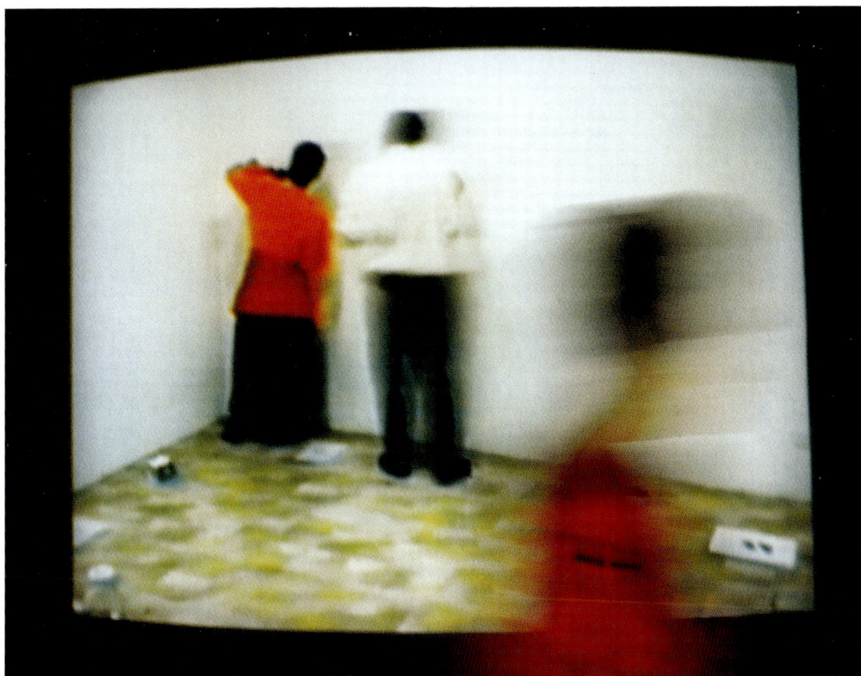

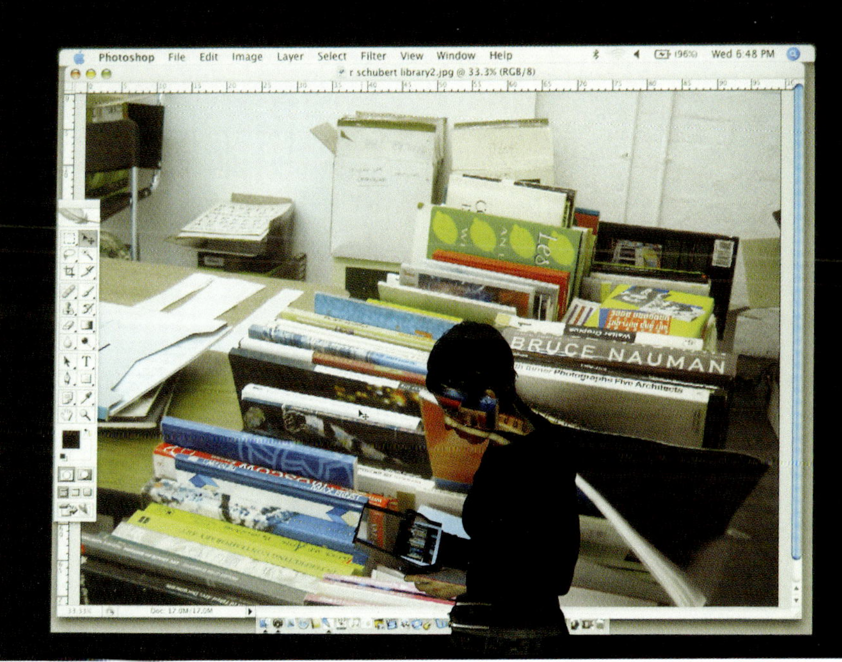
Photoshop File Edit Image Layer Select Filter View Window Help
Wed 6:48 PM
r schubert library2.jpg @ 33.3% (RGB/8)
BRUCE NAUMAN

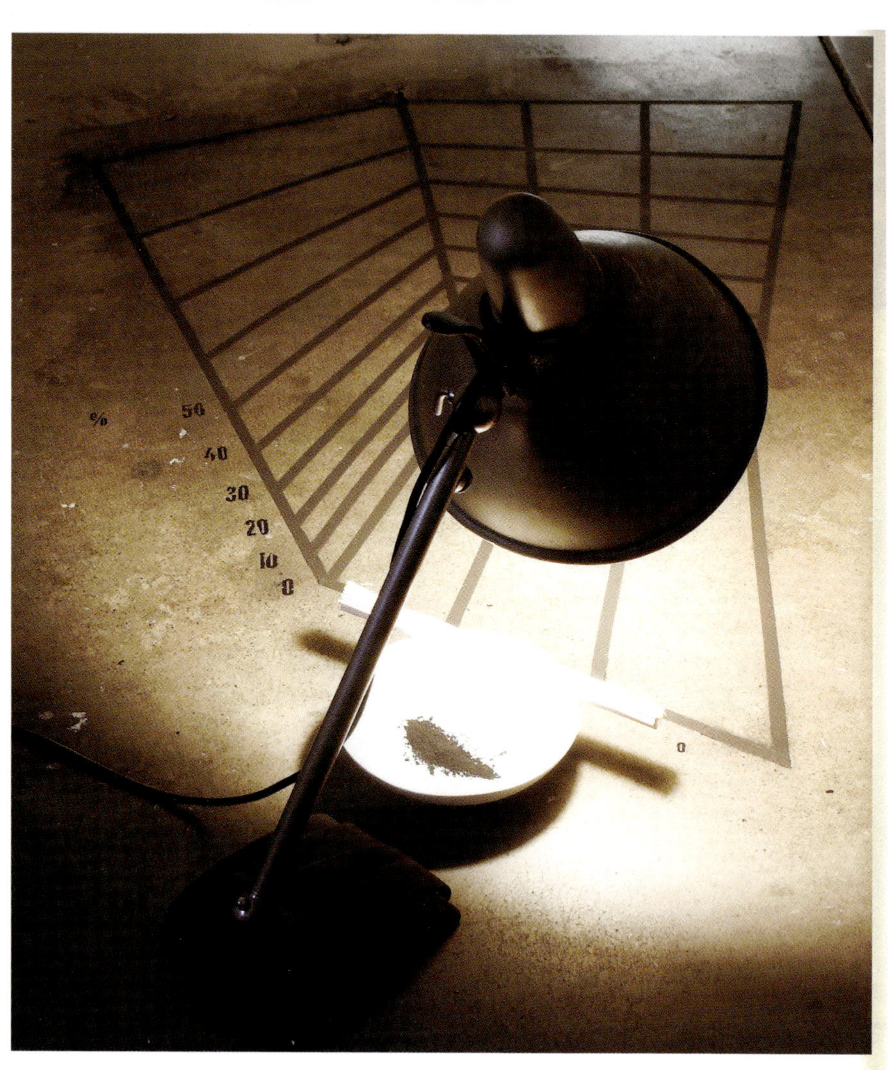

John Abbate
Photo-Graph (detail)
floor drawing comprising photocopier toner, double-sided tape, lamp, bowl, photocopy
2005

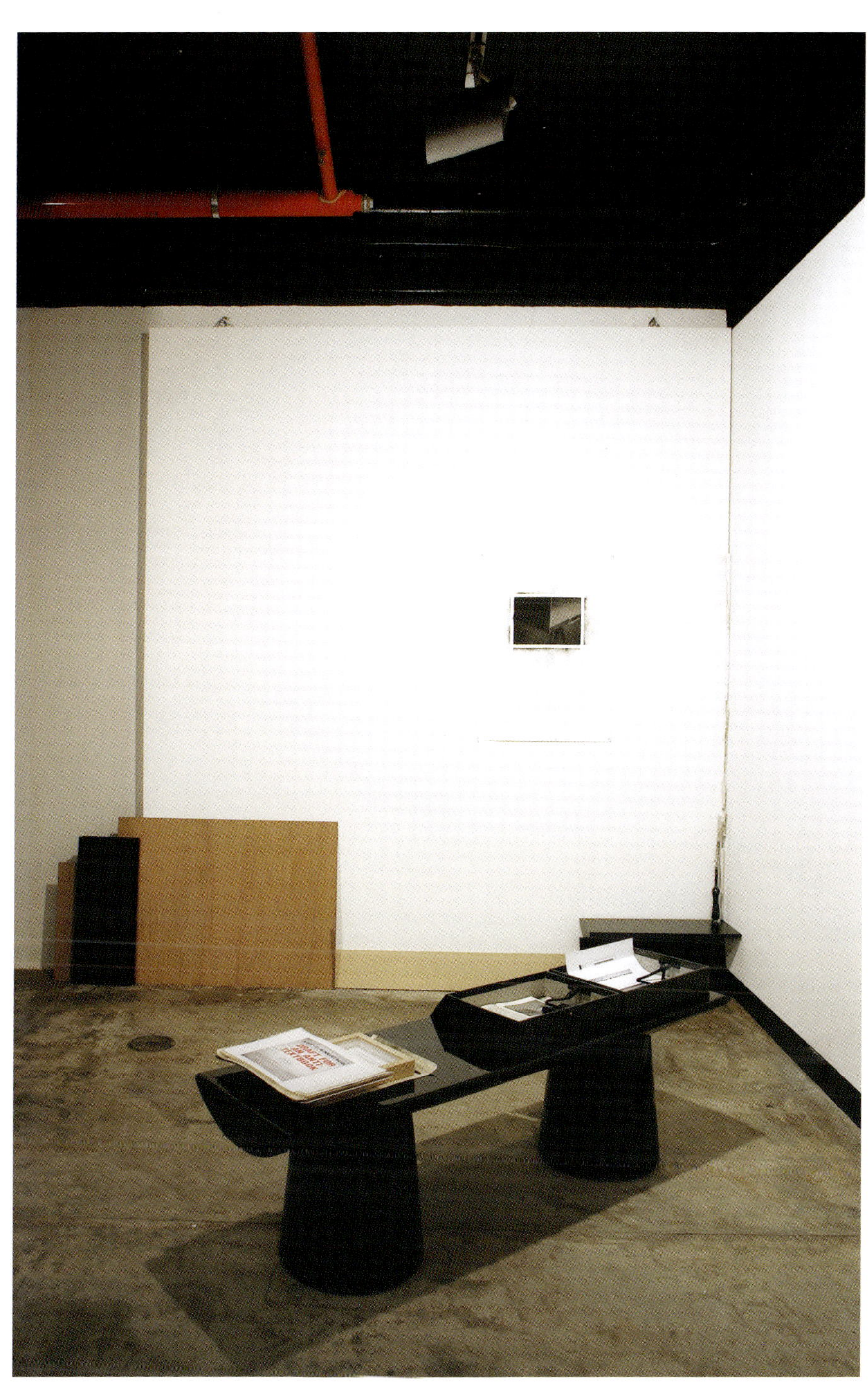

John Abbate
Black Reception (for Old Conceptual Art)
drawing (compressed charcoal on paper) digital prints, books, photocopies, bench, glass bottle, shelf, archive boxes and wood panels
Ocular Lab: 12 at Spacement Gallery
2005

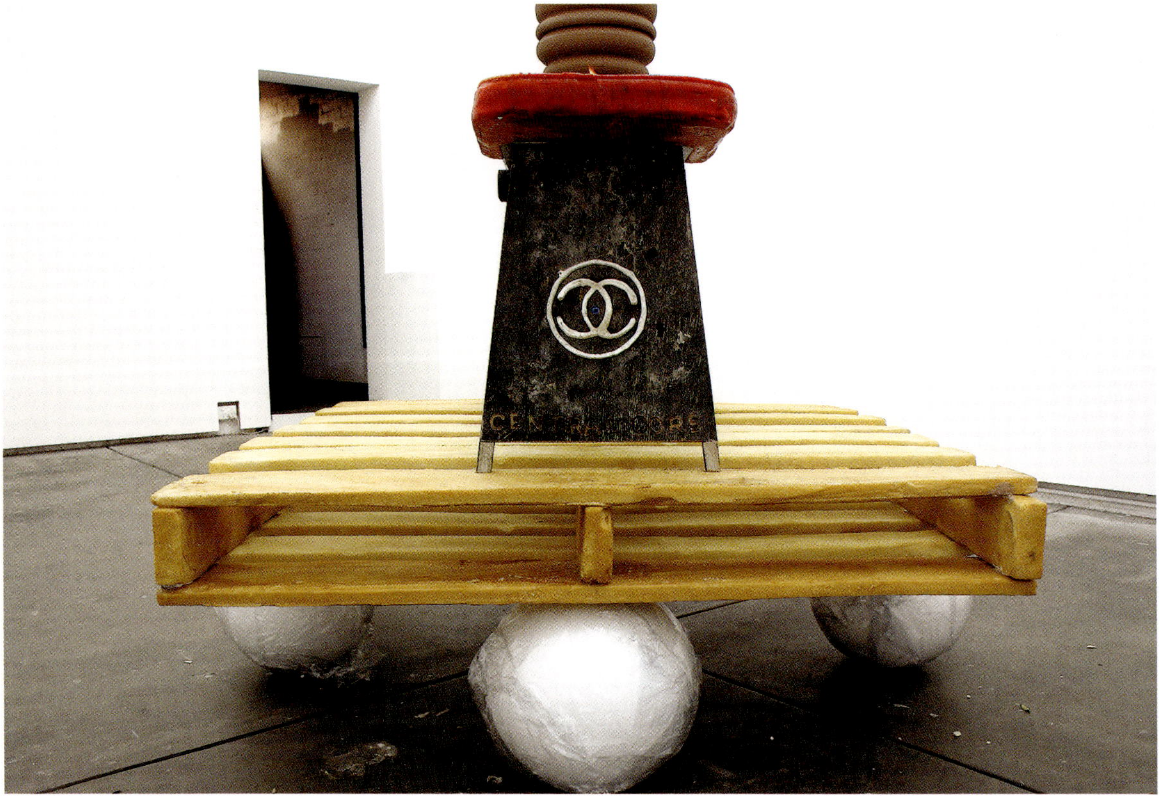

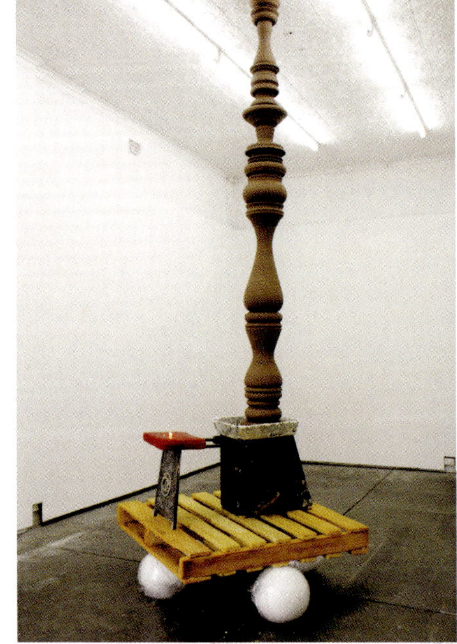

above and right:
Hany Armanious
Central Core Component from Centre of the Universe
installation views
2005
courtesy the artist and Roslyn Oxley9 Gallery

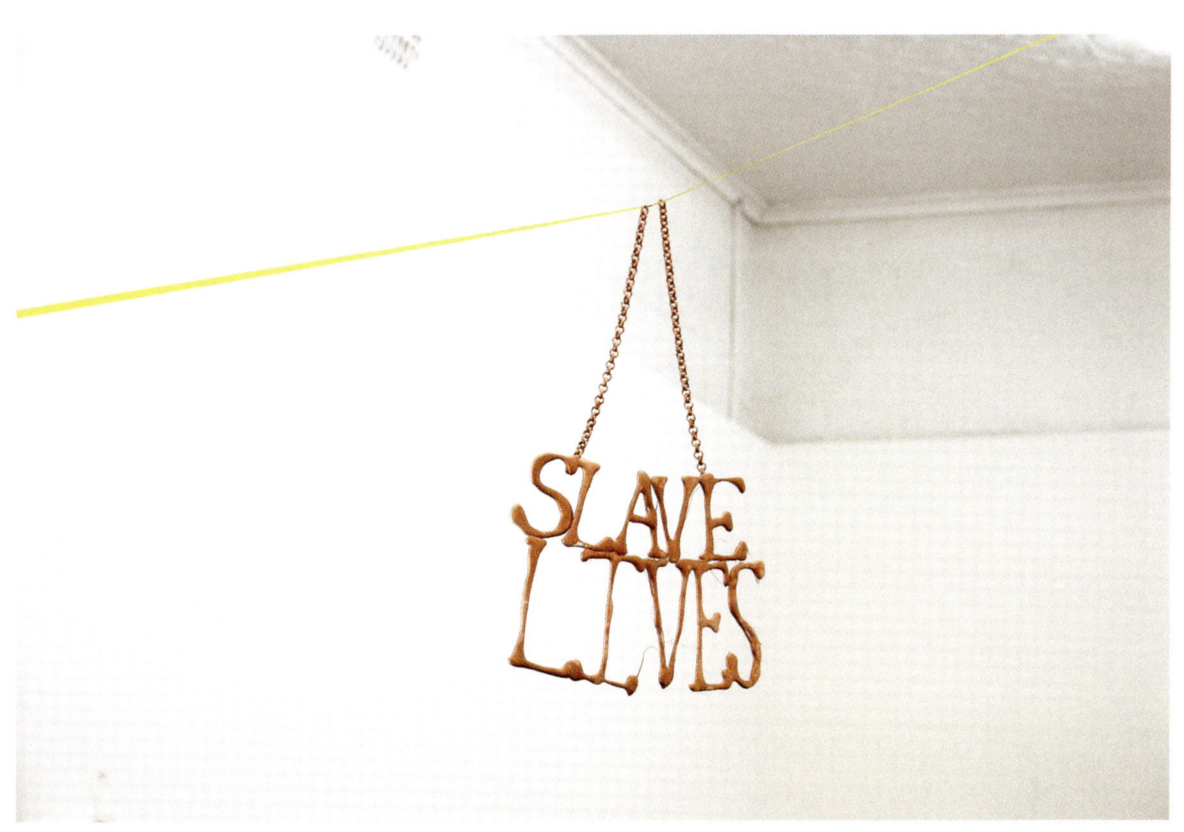

Sarah Goffman
Victoria Victoria!
mixed media, hot glue, found objects
2007

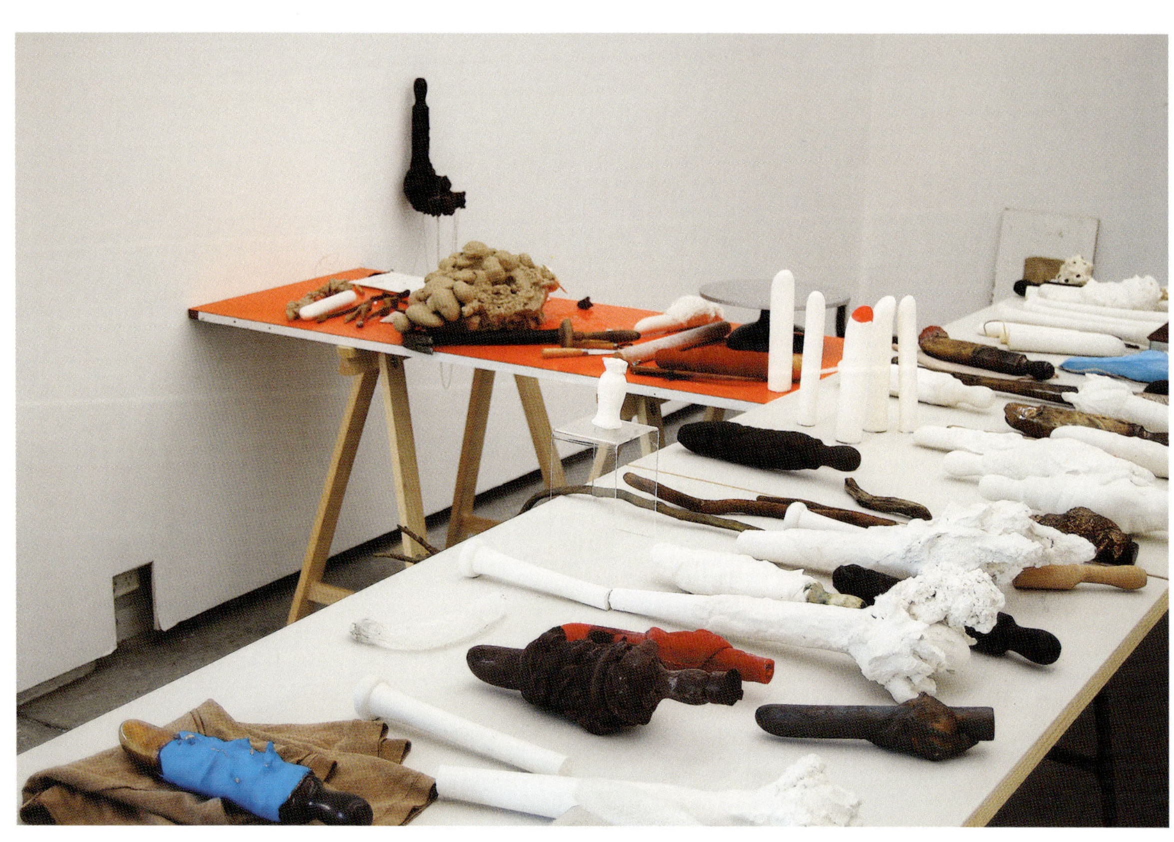

Claire Lambe
Ultra Primo
installation view
part of *Get Oak Firmness*, curated by Elvis Richardson
2009
courtesy the artist and Sarah Scout

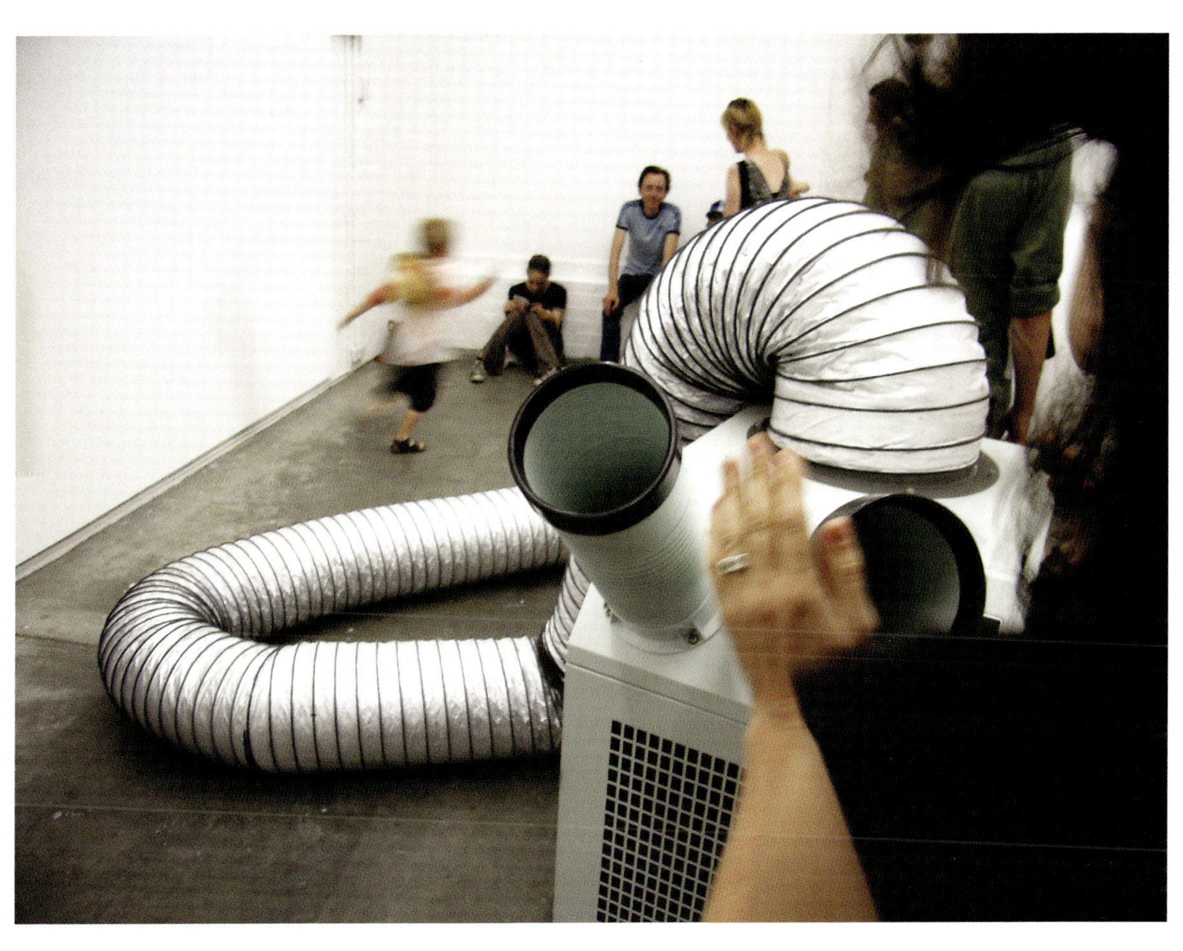

Open Spatial Workshop (OSW-4)
Terri Bird, Bianca Hester, Natasha Johns-Messenger, Scott Mitchell
Active Air
functioning industrial cooler
2005

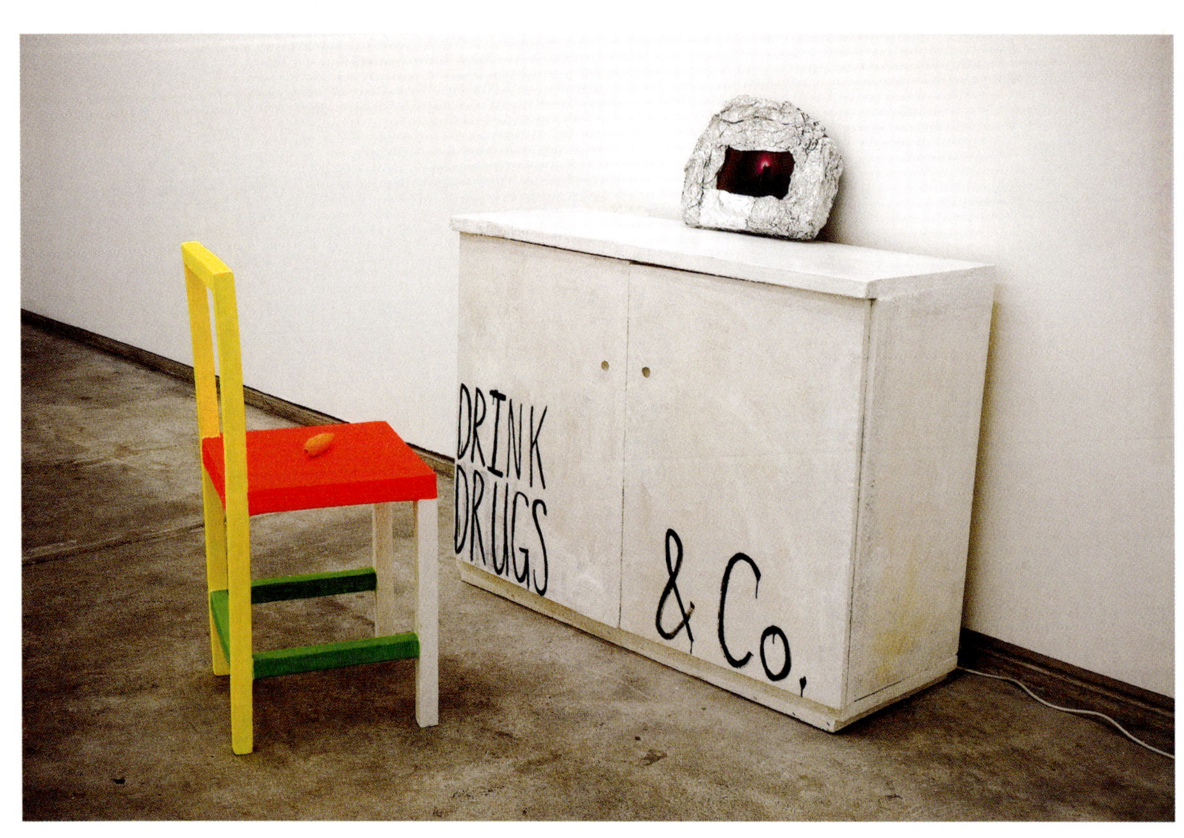

Ronnie van Hout
Fallenness
installation view
2009
photograph: Ronnie van Hout
courtesy the artist and Kaliman Rawlins (Melbourne), Darren Knight (Sydney), Hamish McKay (Wellington), and Ivan Anthony (Auckland)

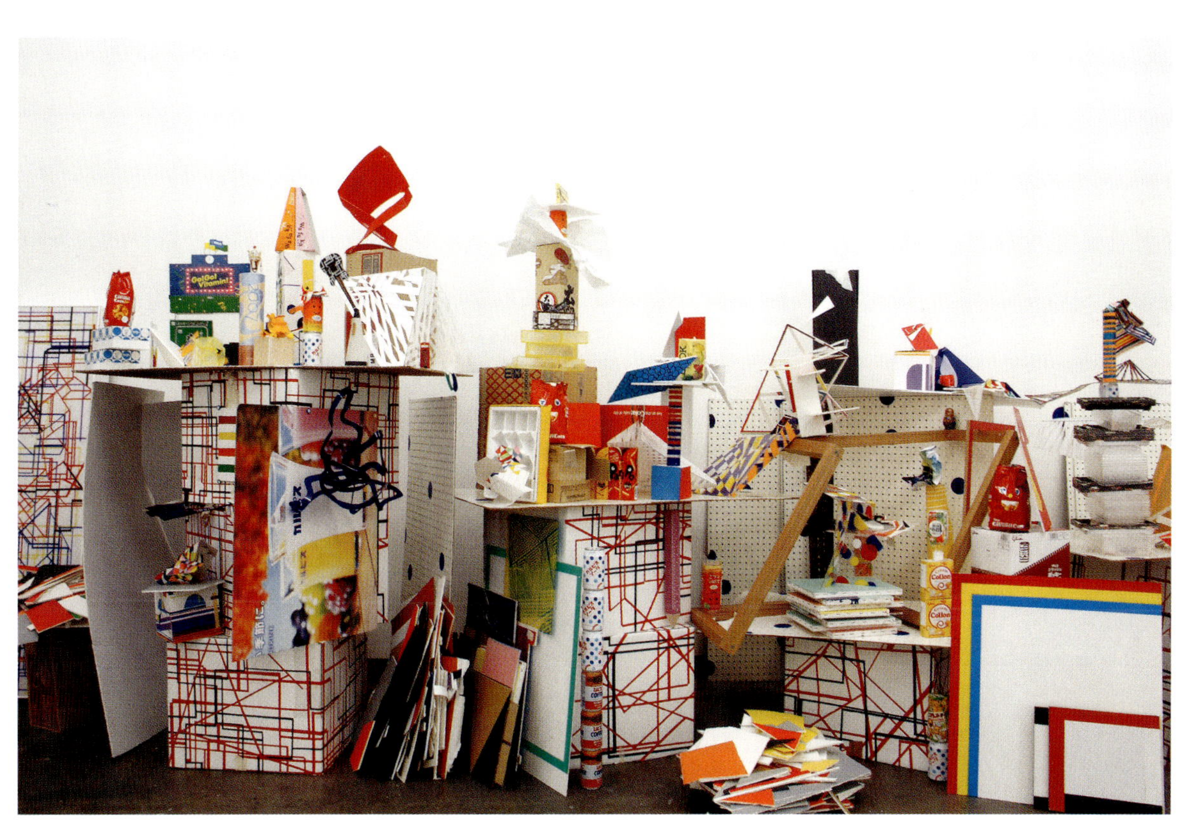

Masato Takasaka
I Like My Old Stuff Better Than Your New Stuff
(More prog rock sculptures from the 5th dimension)
installation: mixed media
2007

Susan Jacobs
For Every Solution There Is A Problem
tree trunks, plaster wall and wooden door
2007
courtesy the artist and Sarah Scout

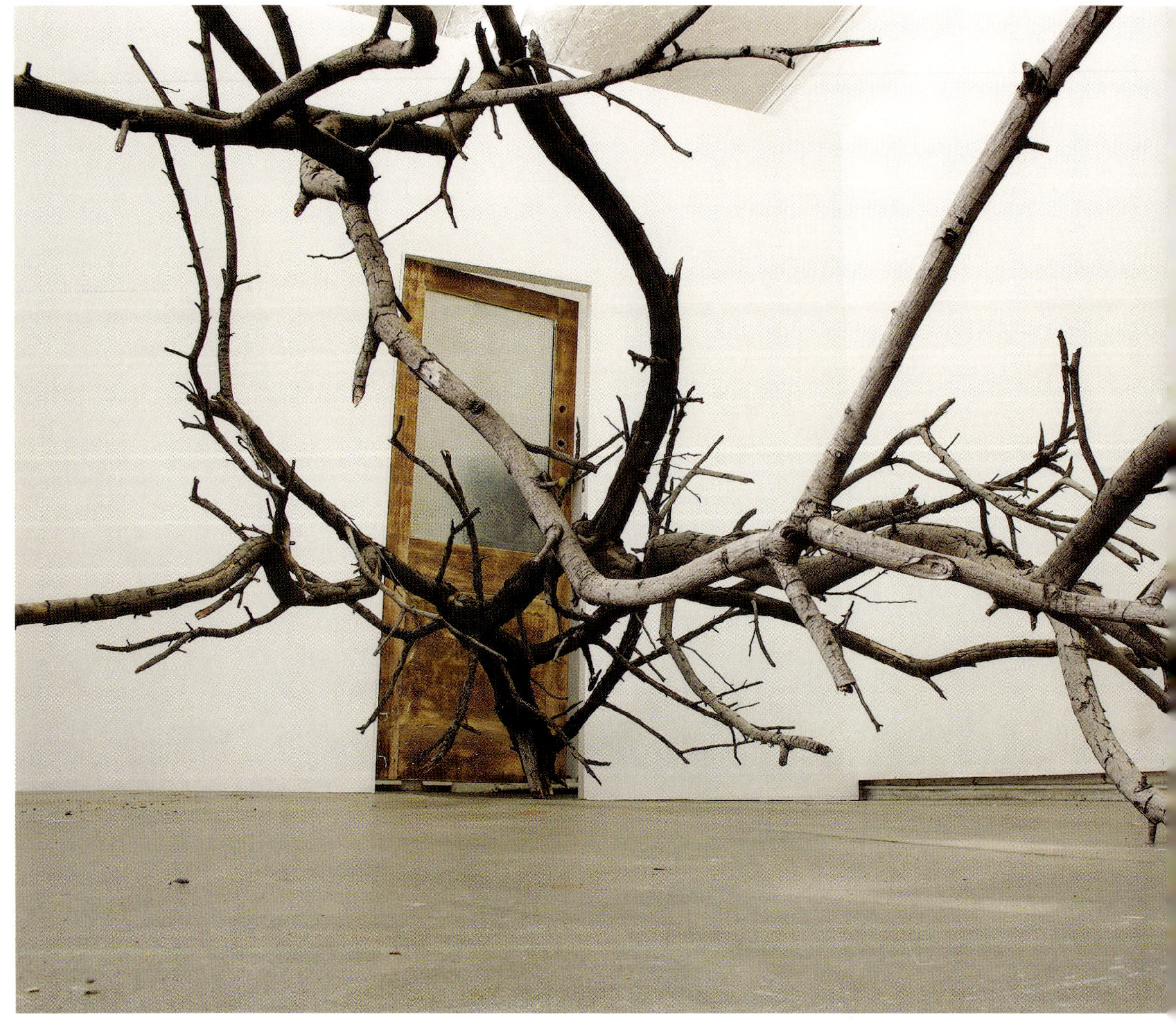

Julie Davies
Dismantle #7
video stills from the *Dismantle* series
Ocular Notes at George Paton Gallery, Melbourne
2007
courtesy the artist and Place Gallery

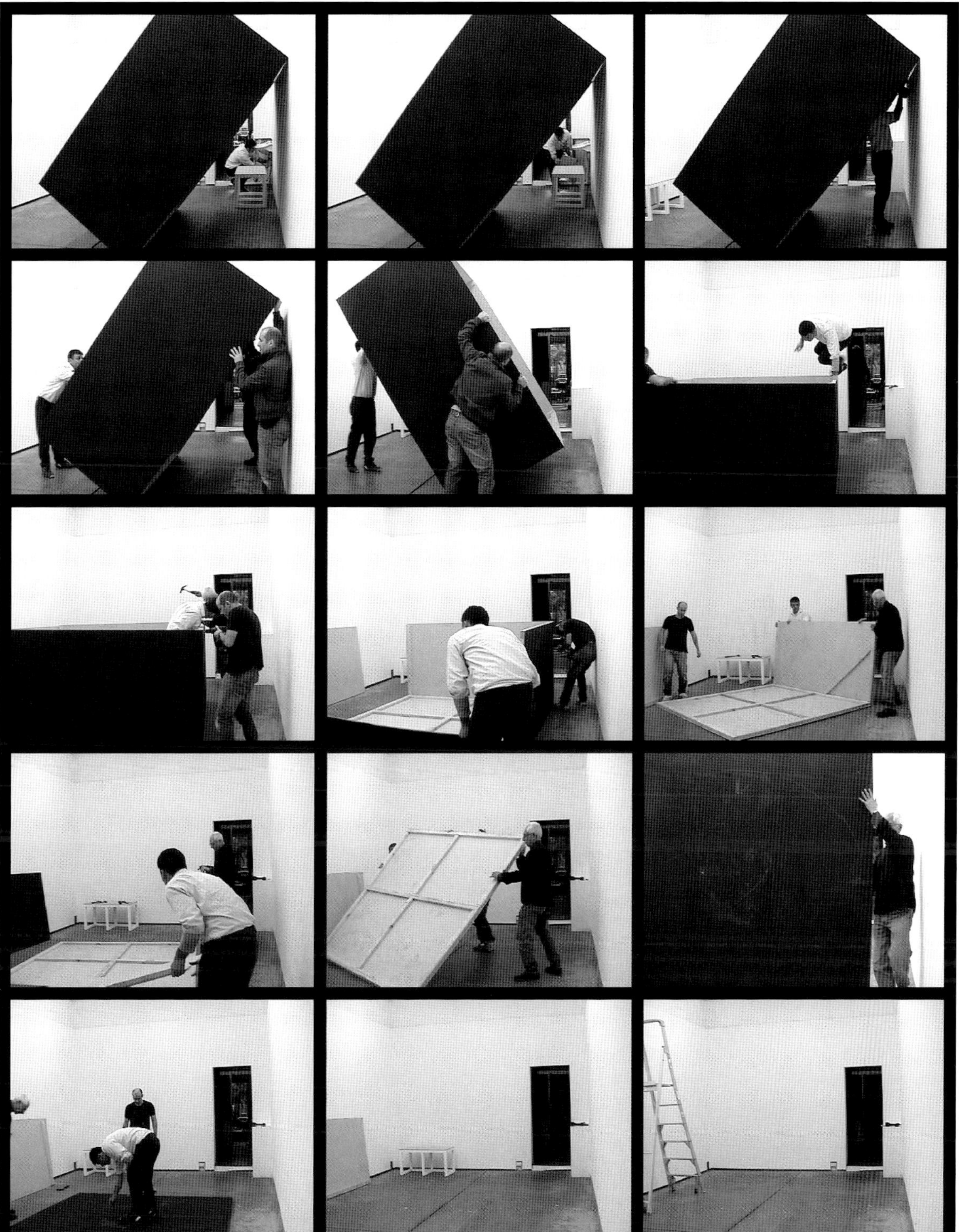

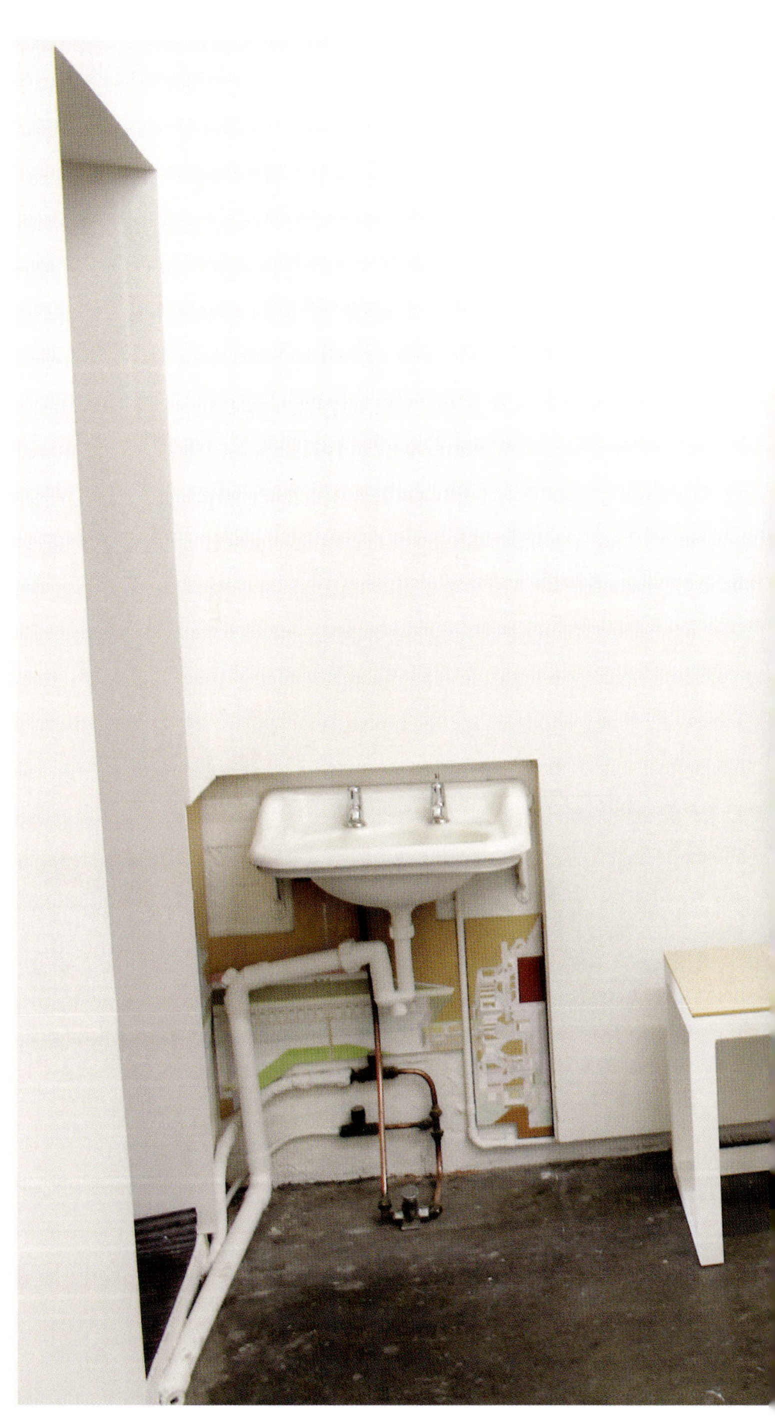

Raafat Ishak
Apparition of a Miserable Acquaintance
acrylic paint on MDF and wood
2005
courtesy the artist and Sutton Gallery

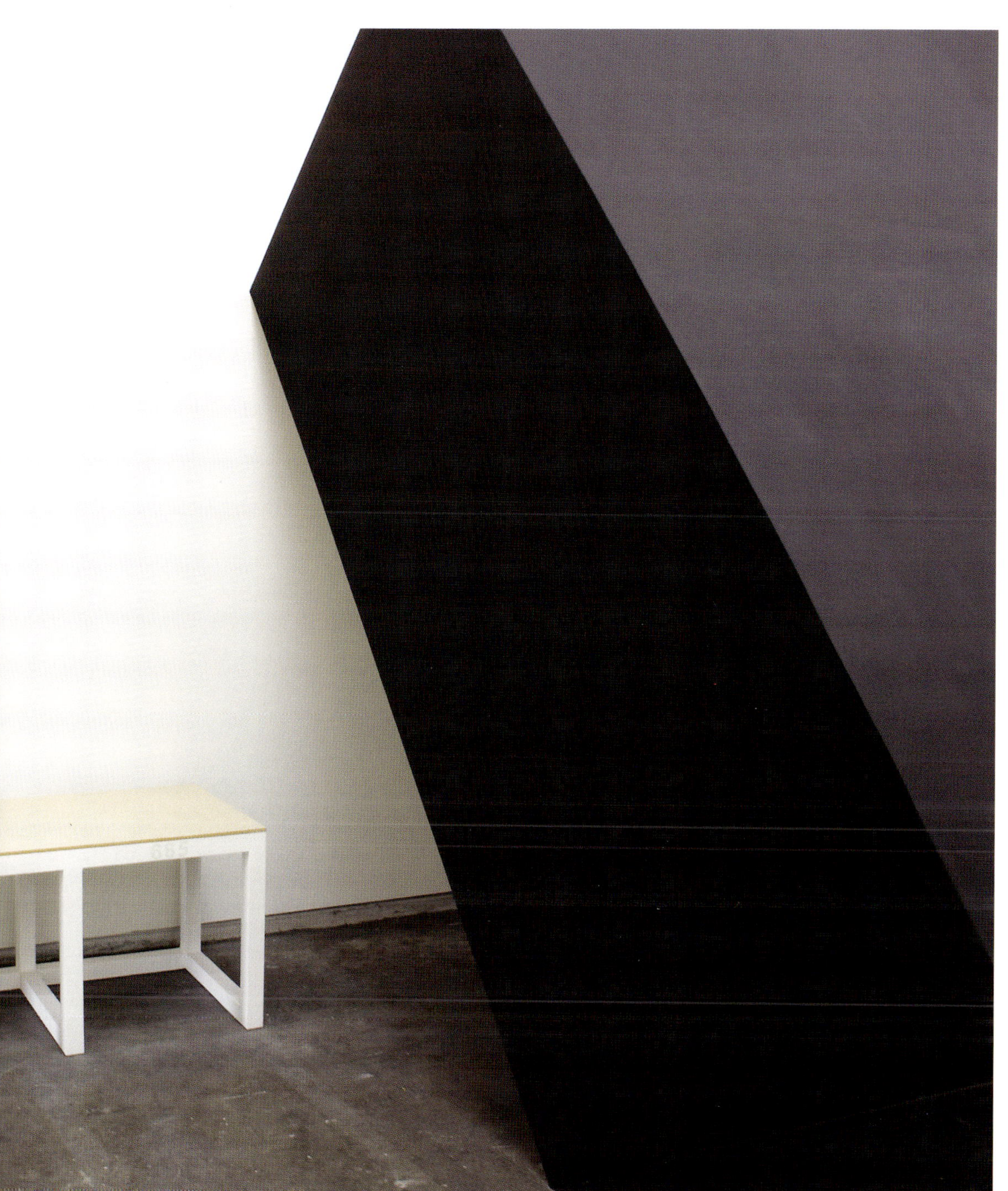

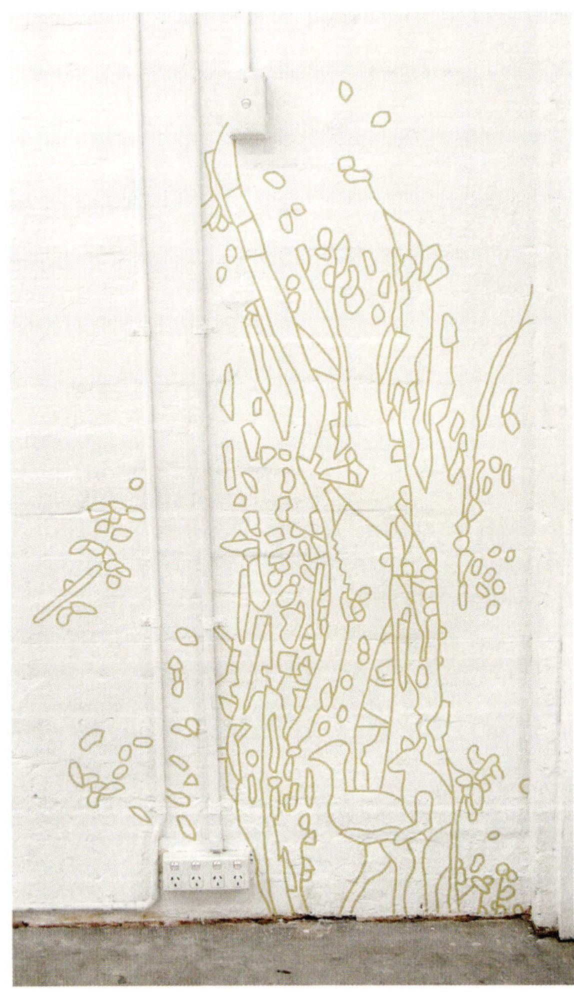

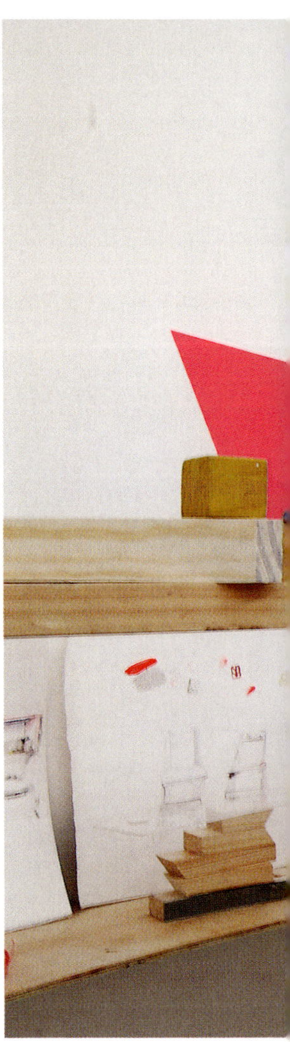

Raafat Ishak
Untitled
acrylic paint on wall
2004
courtesy the artist and Sutton Gallery

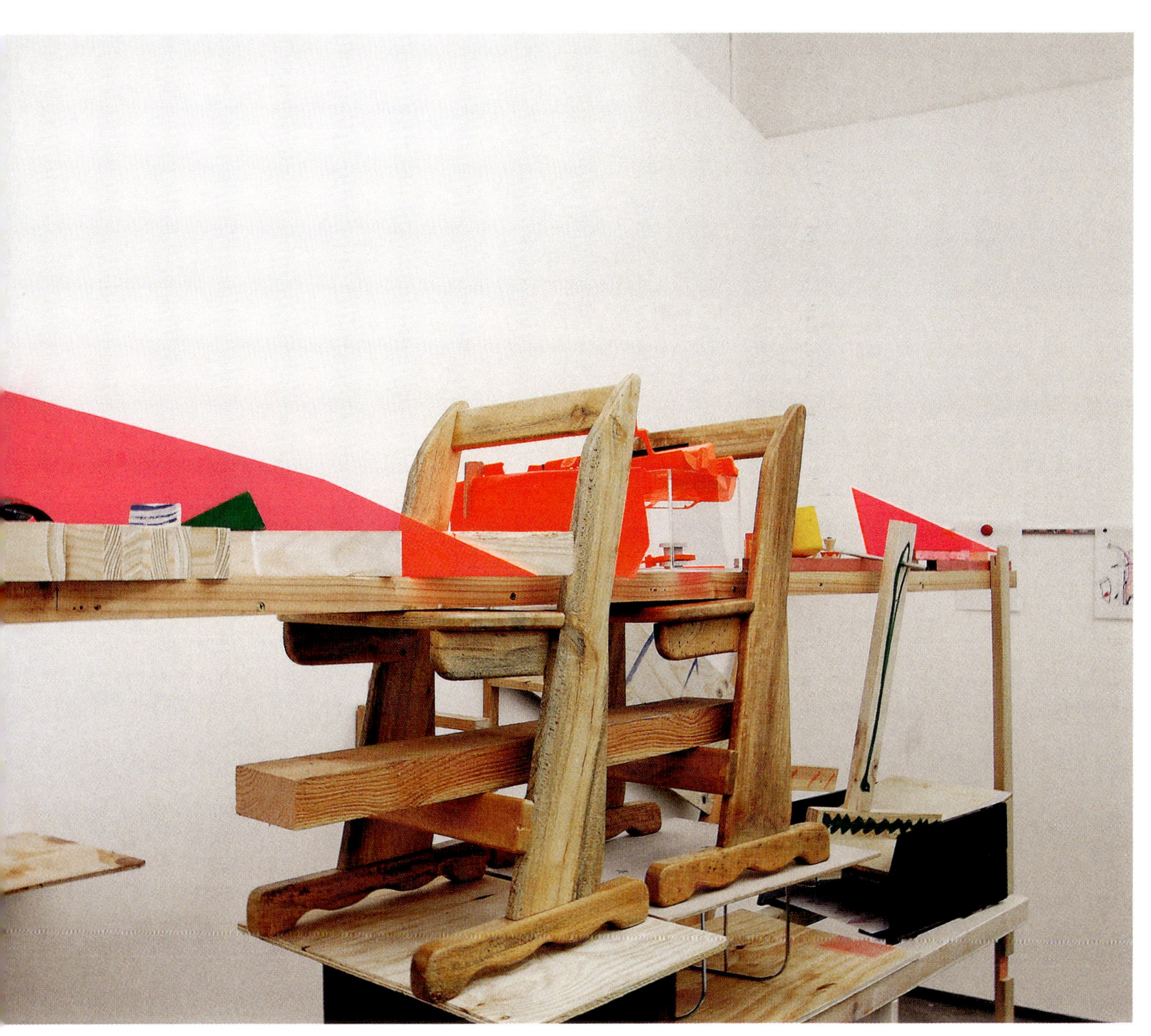

Katherine Huang
Assemblages and Drawings
mixed media construction
2006
courtesy the artist and Neon Parc

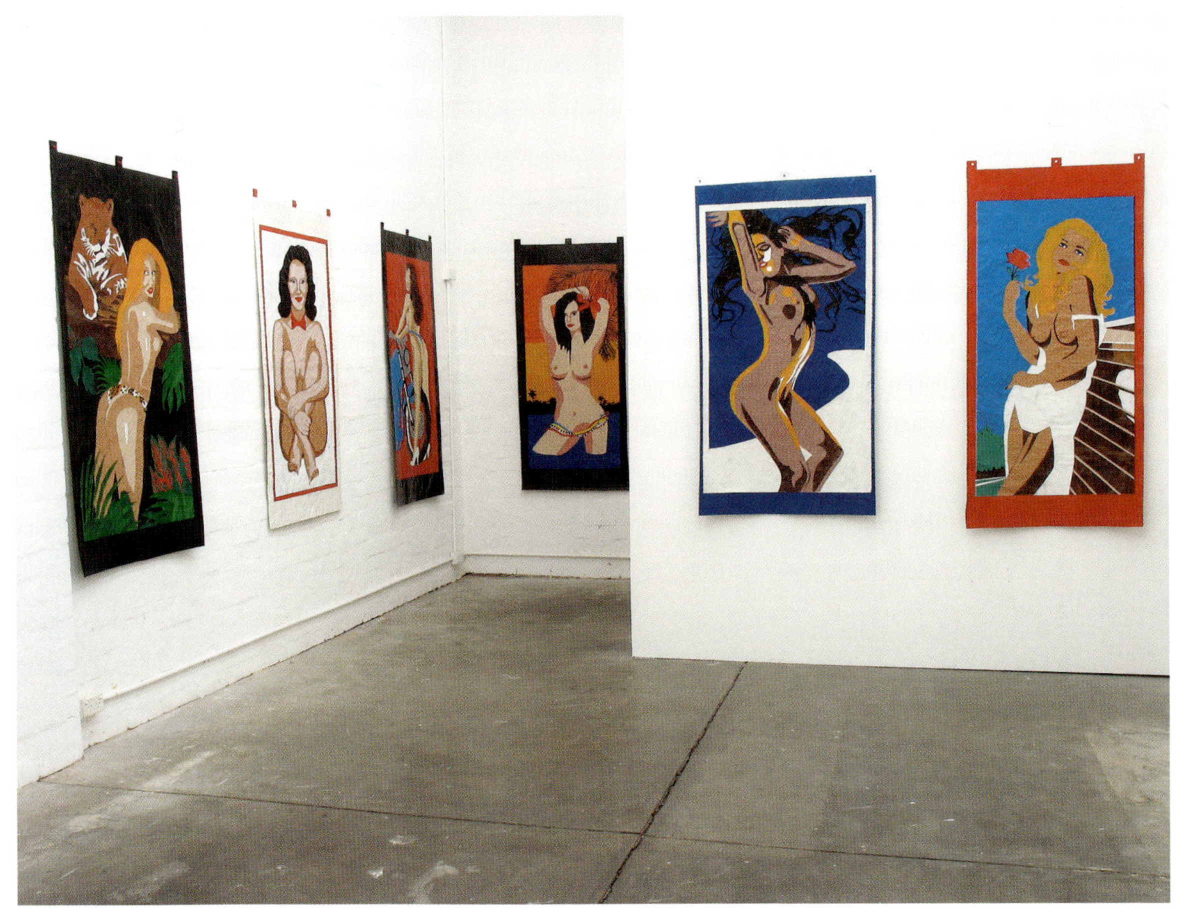

above:
Louise Paramor
Mädchen Club and 'other stuff'
paintings/collage
2004
courtesy the artist and Nellie Castan Gallery

opposite:
Mark Shorter
Renny Kodgers 'The Model'
performance at Ocular Lab
part of *Get Oak Firmness,* curated by Elvis Richardson
2009

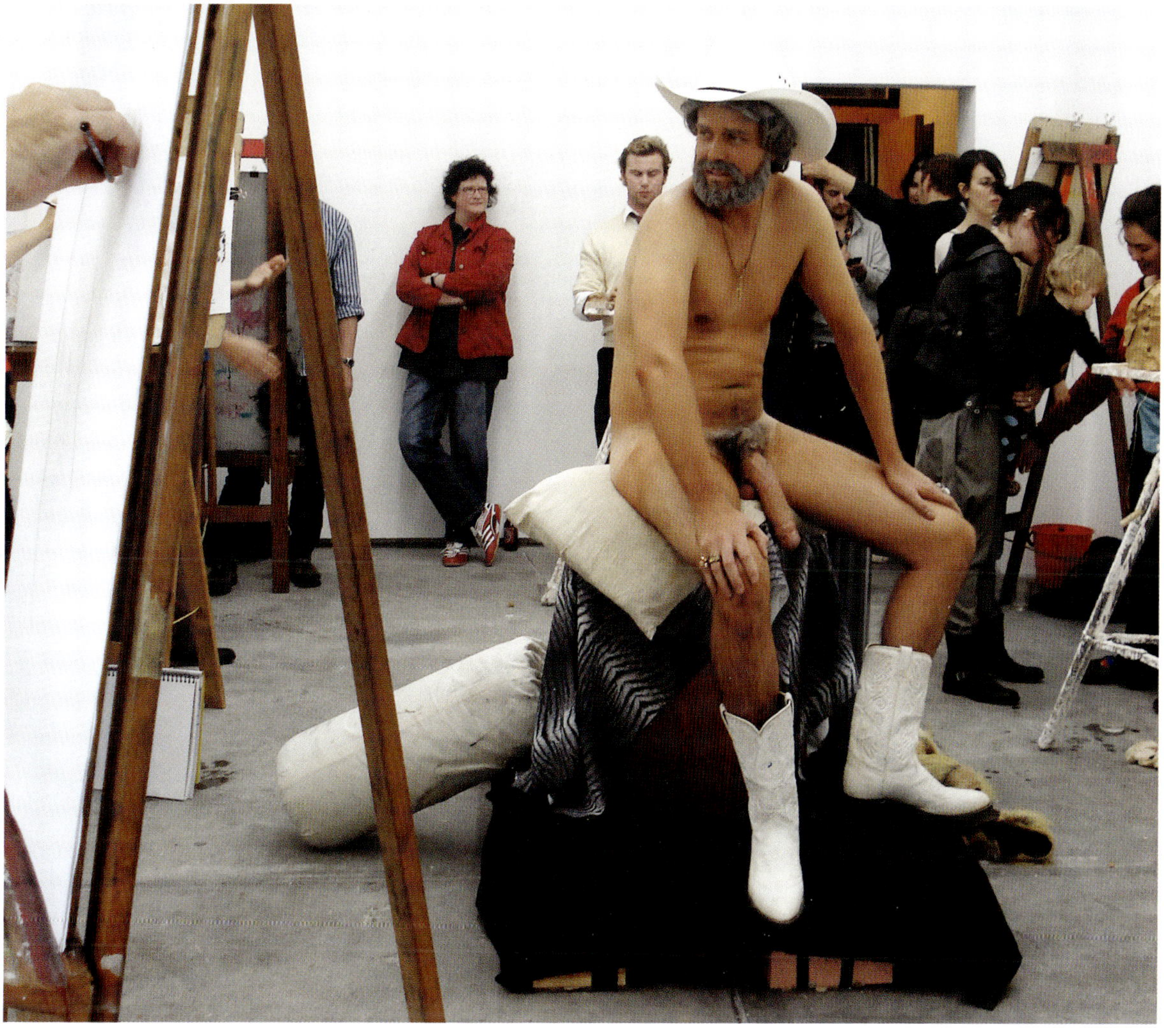

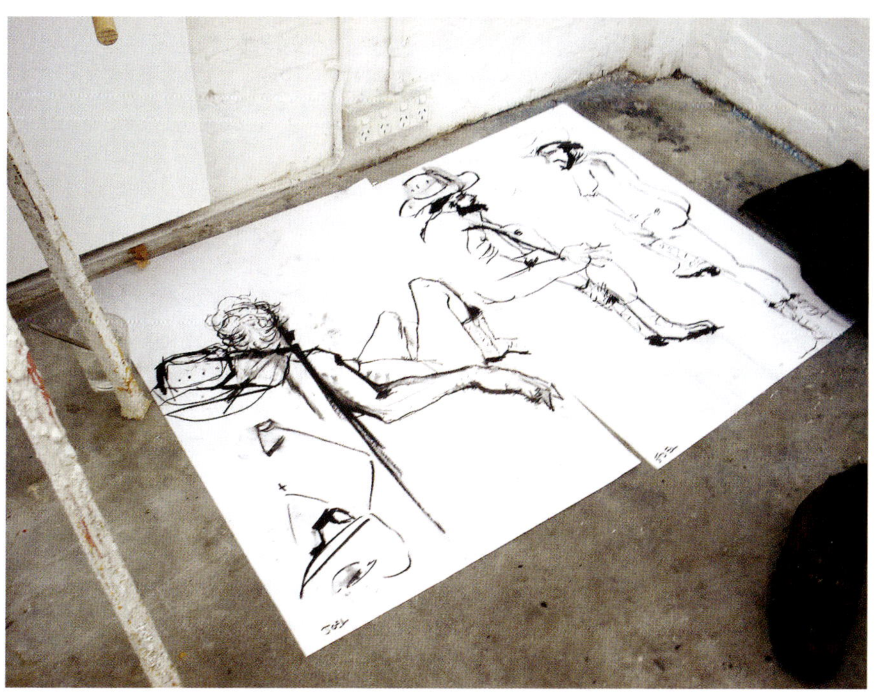

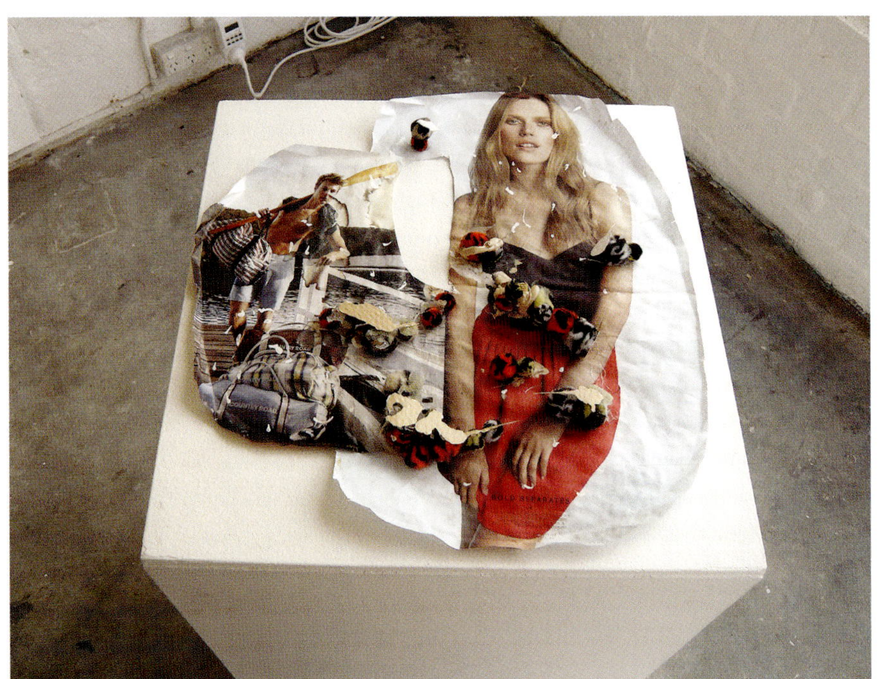

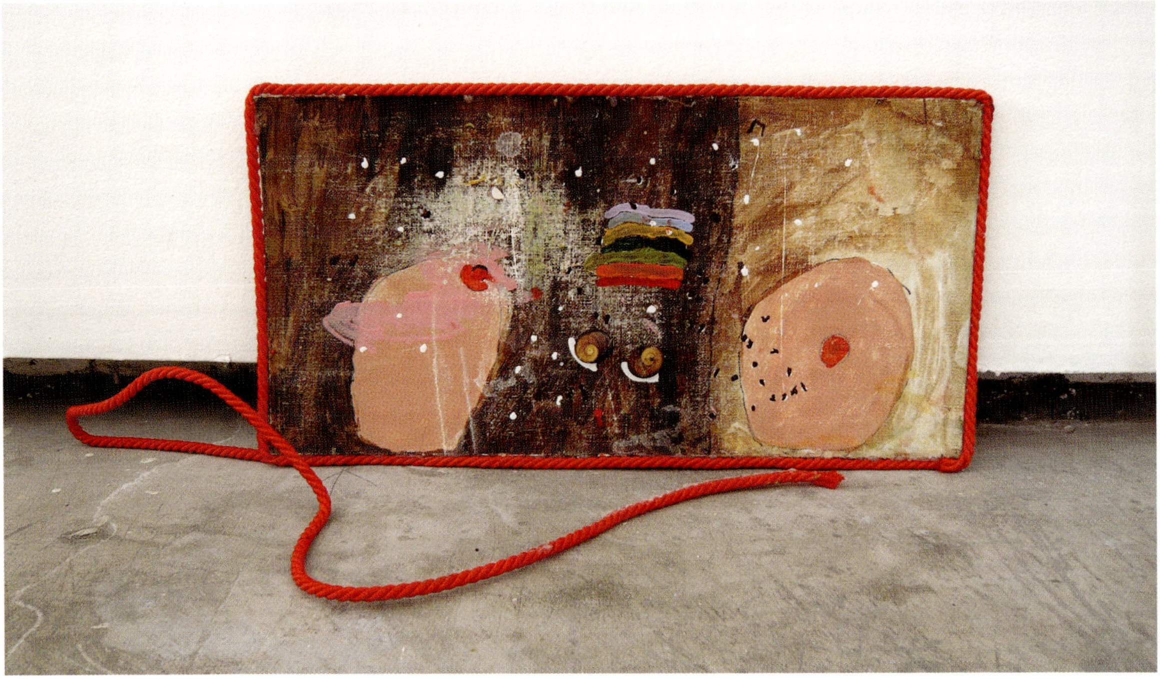

top:
Kate Smith
polo ralph lauren, country road and fluff
magazines, acrylic and fluffy balls
2009
courtesy the artist and Sutton Gallery

bottom:
Kate Smith
boobs 2009
oil, acrylic and rope on canvas board
2009
courtesy the artist and Sutton Gallery

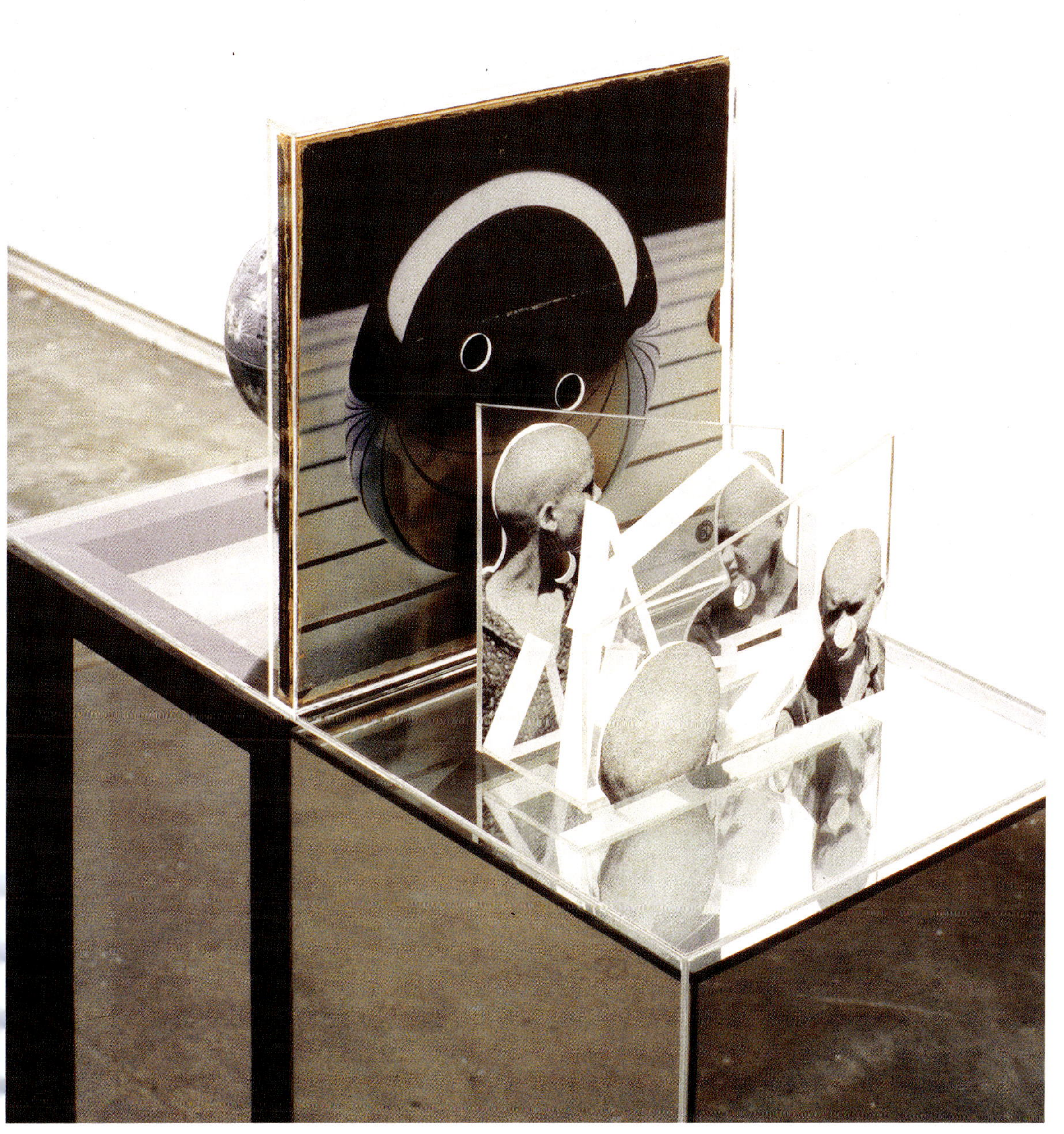

Damiano Bertoli
The faster we go, the rounder we get
mixed media
2005
courtesy the artist and Neon Parc

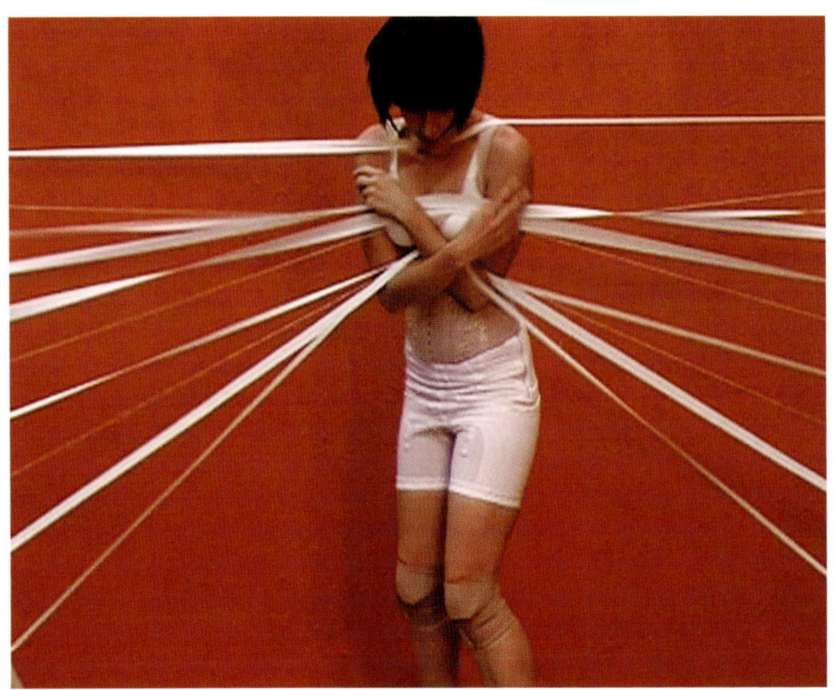

above:
Kellie Wells
The Joy of Living
video still
2009

opposite top:
Andrew Hurle
Lady Smoking
inkjet print on archival paper
2004

opposite below:
Eliza Hutchinson
from the series *The Entertainers 2*
pegasus print
2004

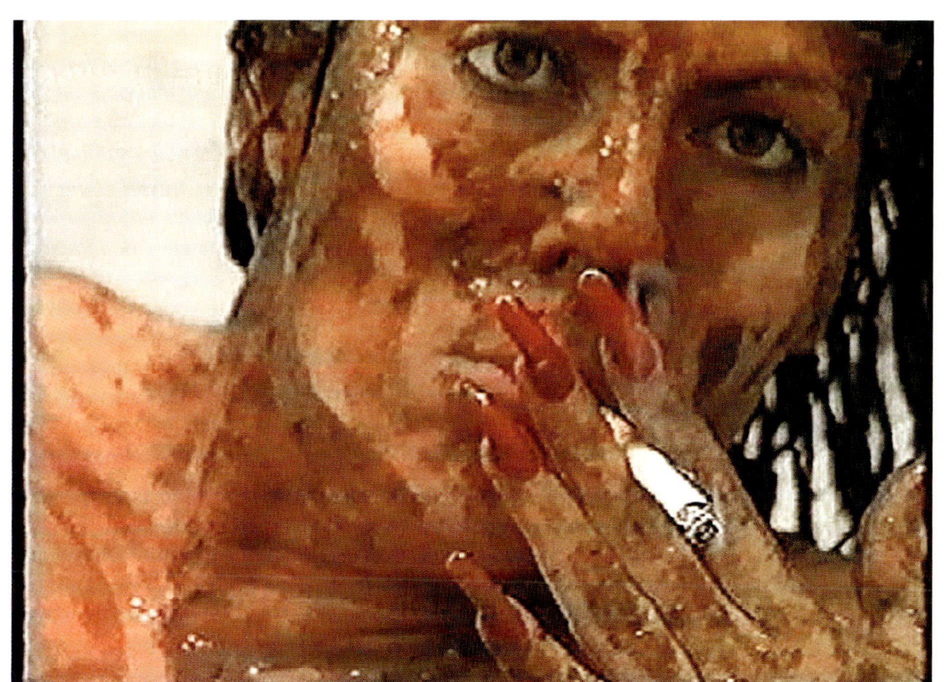

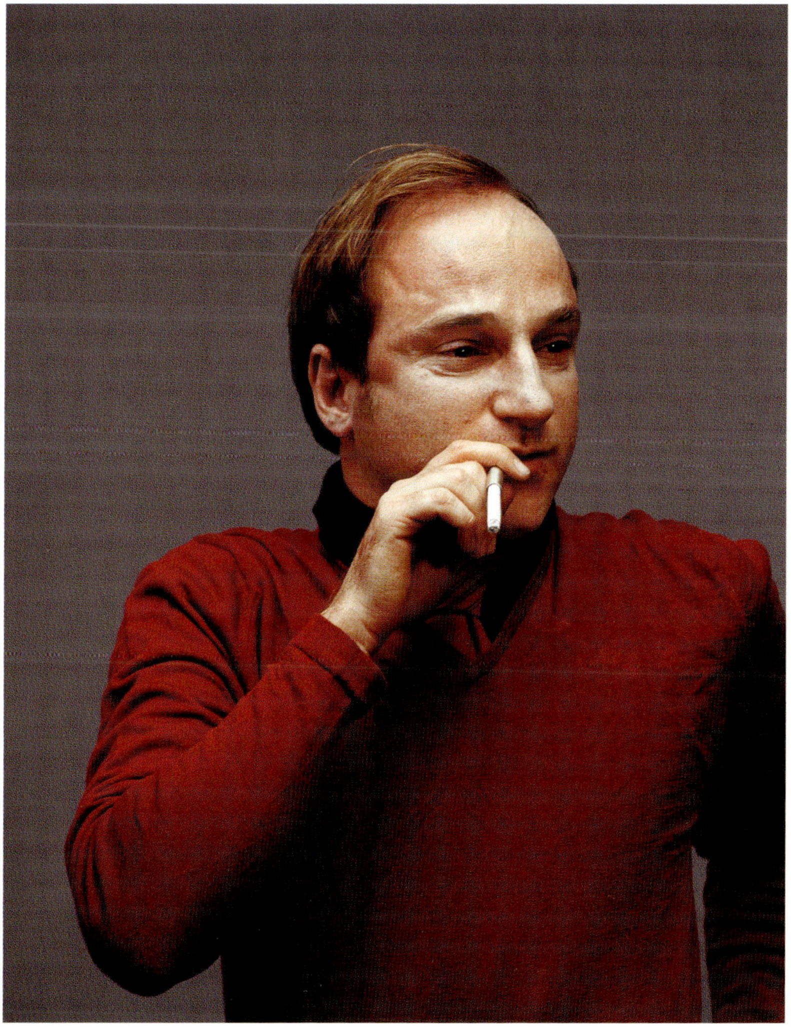

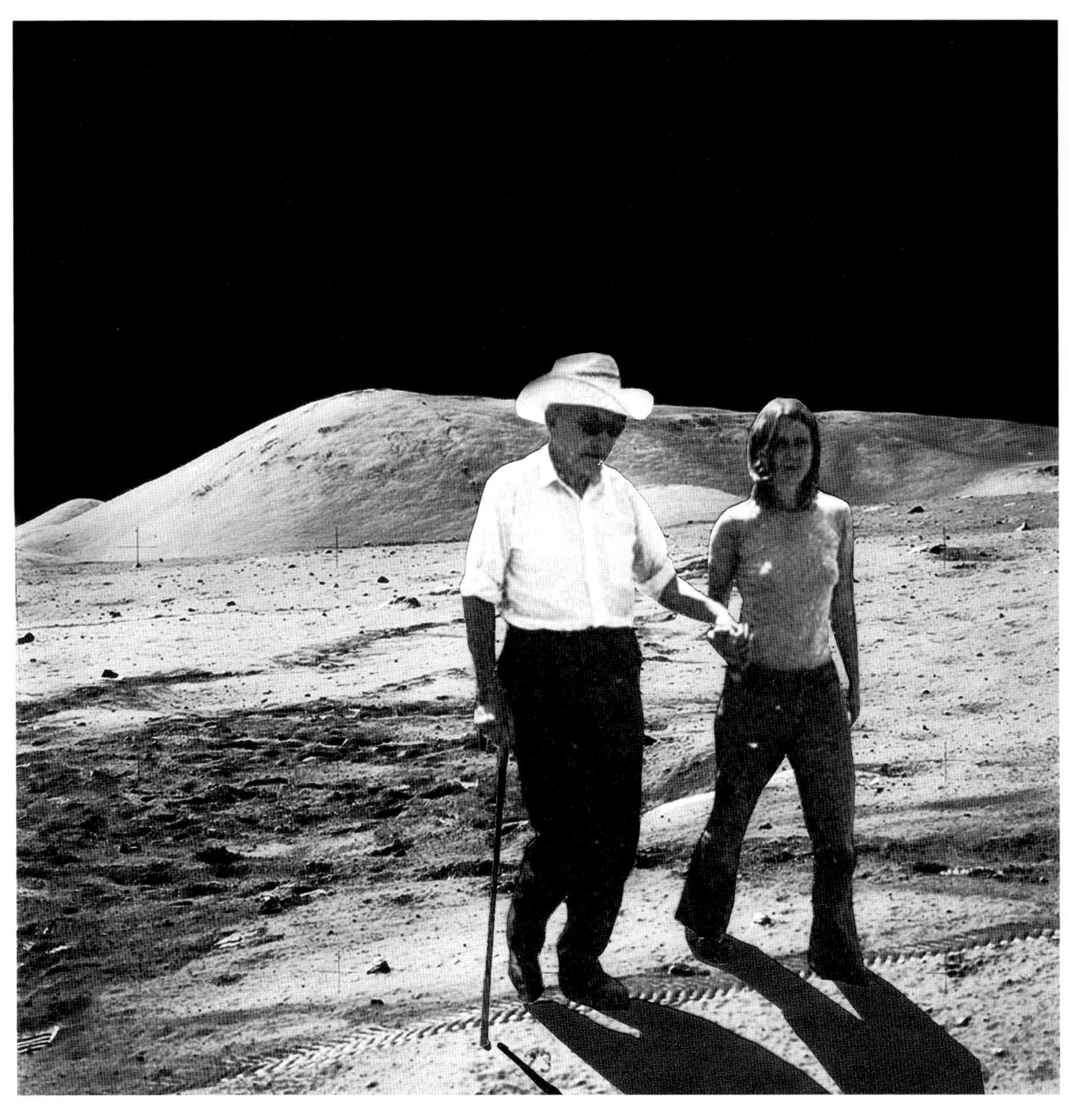

above and opposite:
Damiano Bertoli
Continuous Moment: Whiteys on the Moon
digital prints on canvas
Trinity Nine at Trinity College, The University of Melbourne
2006
courtesy the artist and Neon Parc

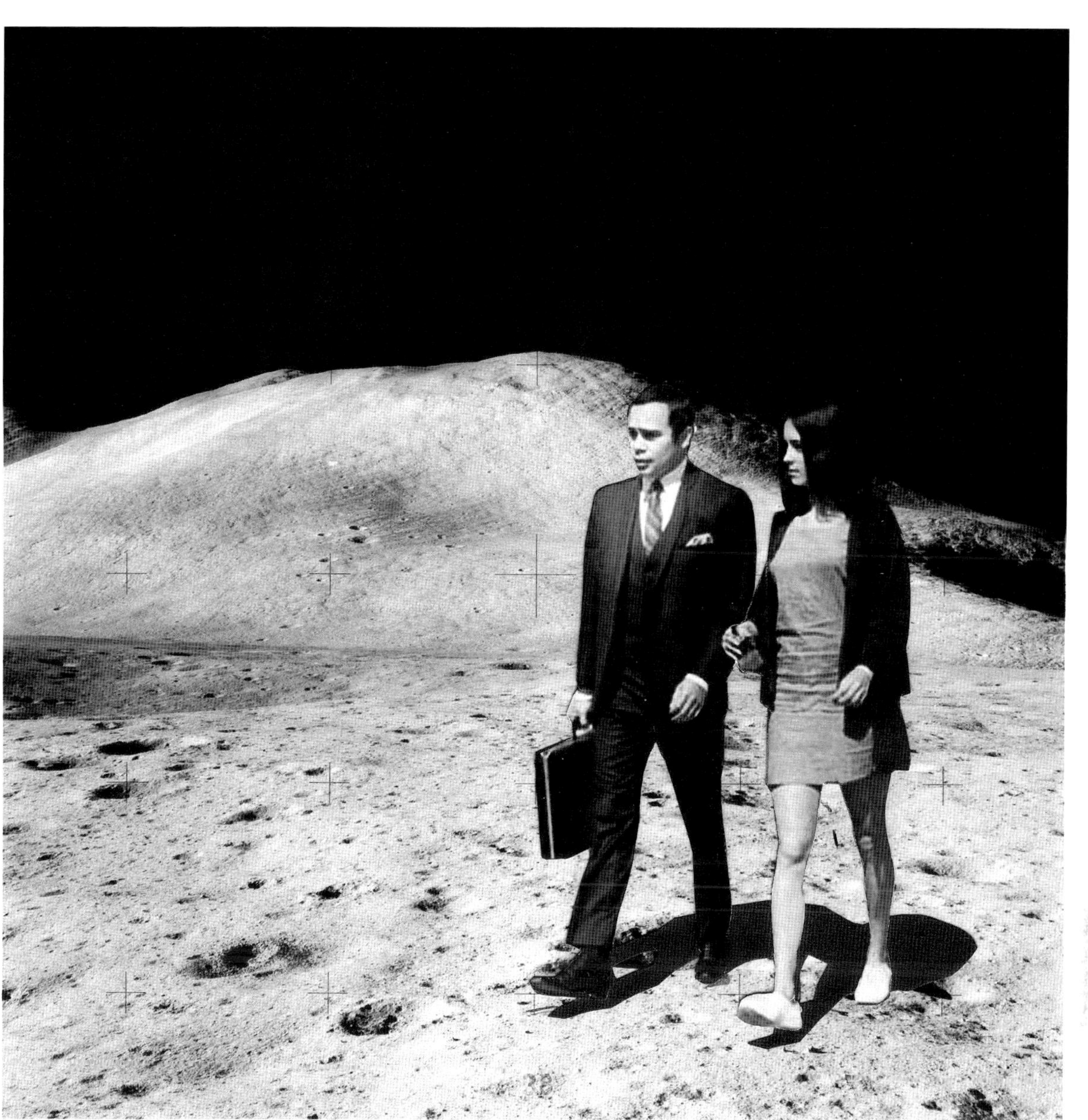

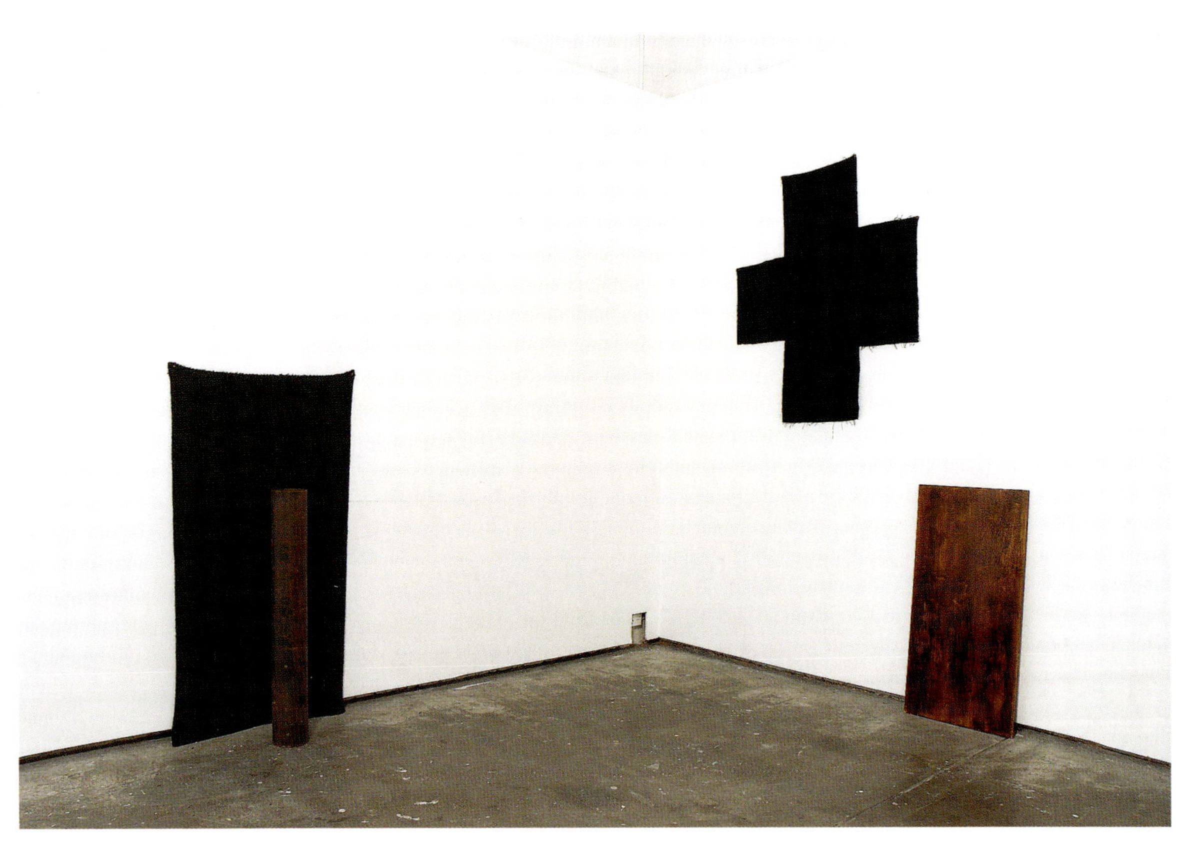

above and opposite:
Elizabeth Newman
The Unprecedented Dark Light of the New Letters
mixed media (fabric, wood, metal, rubber, framed photocopy)
2007
courtesy the artist and Neon Parc

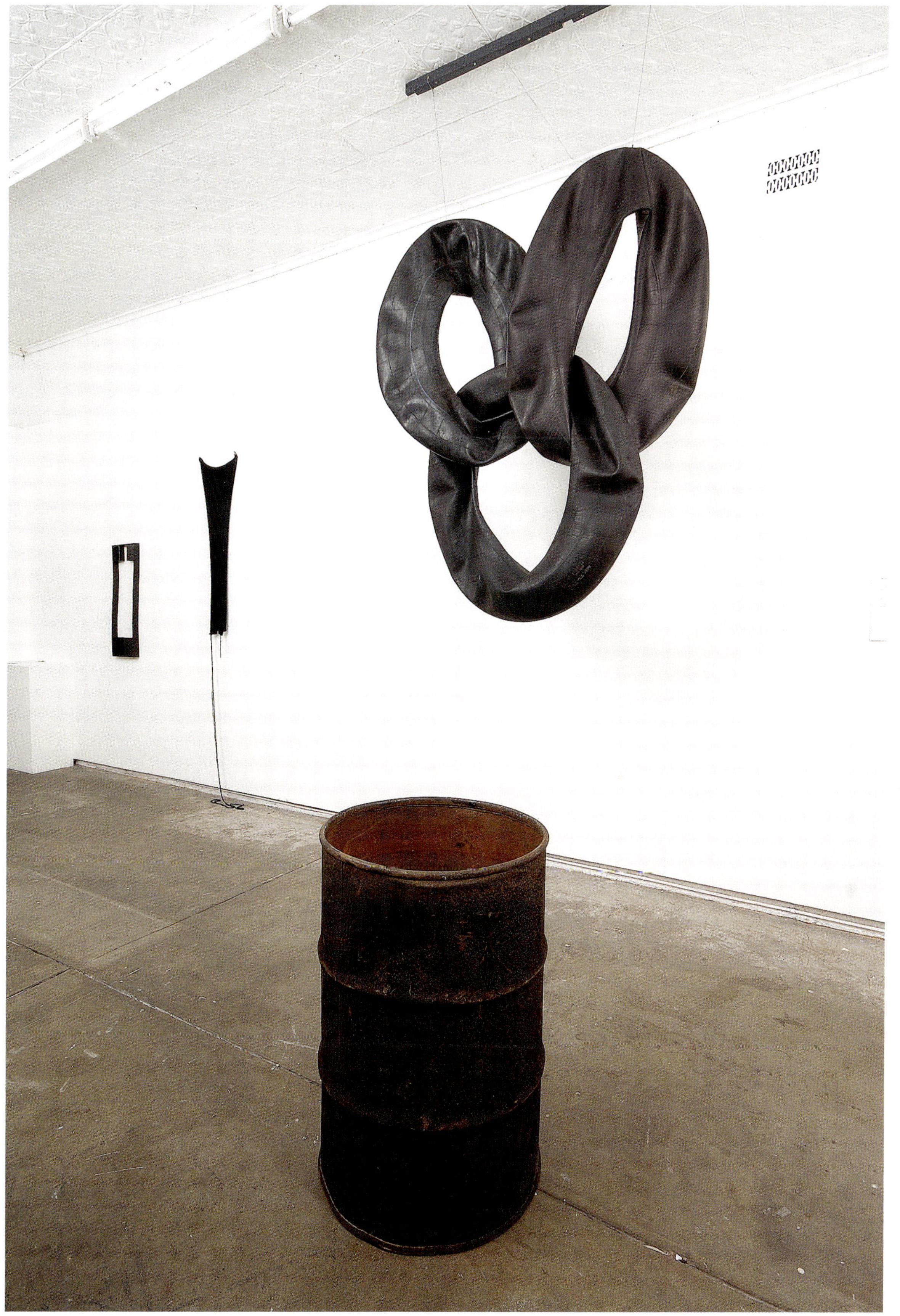

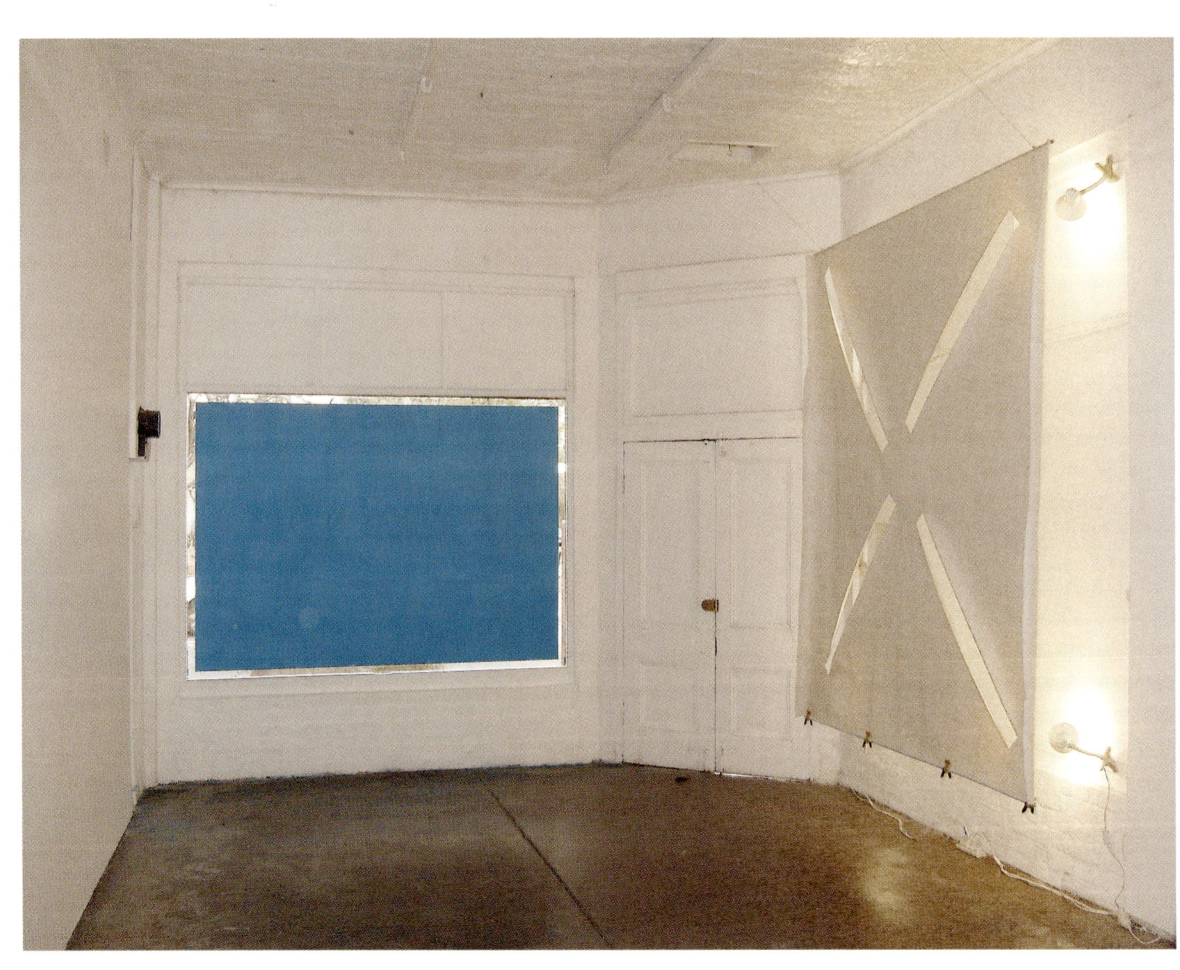

Sean Loughrey and William Seeto
Site Projects
installation project, mixed media
2008
photograph: William Seeto

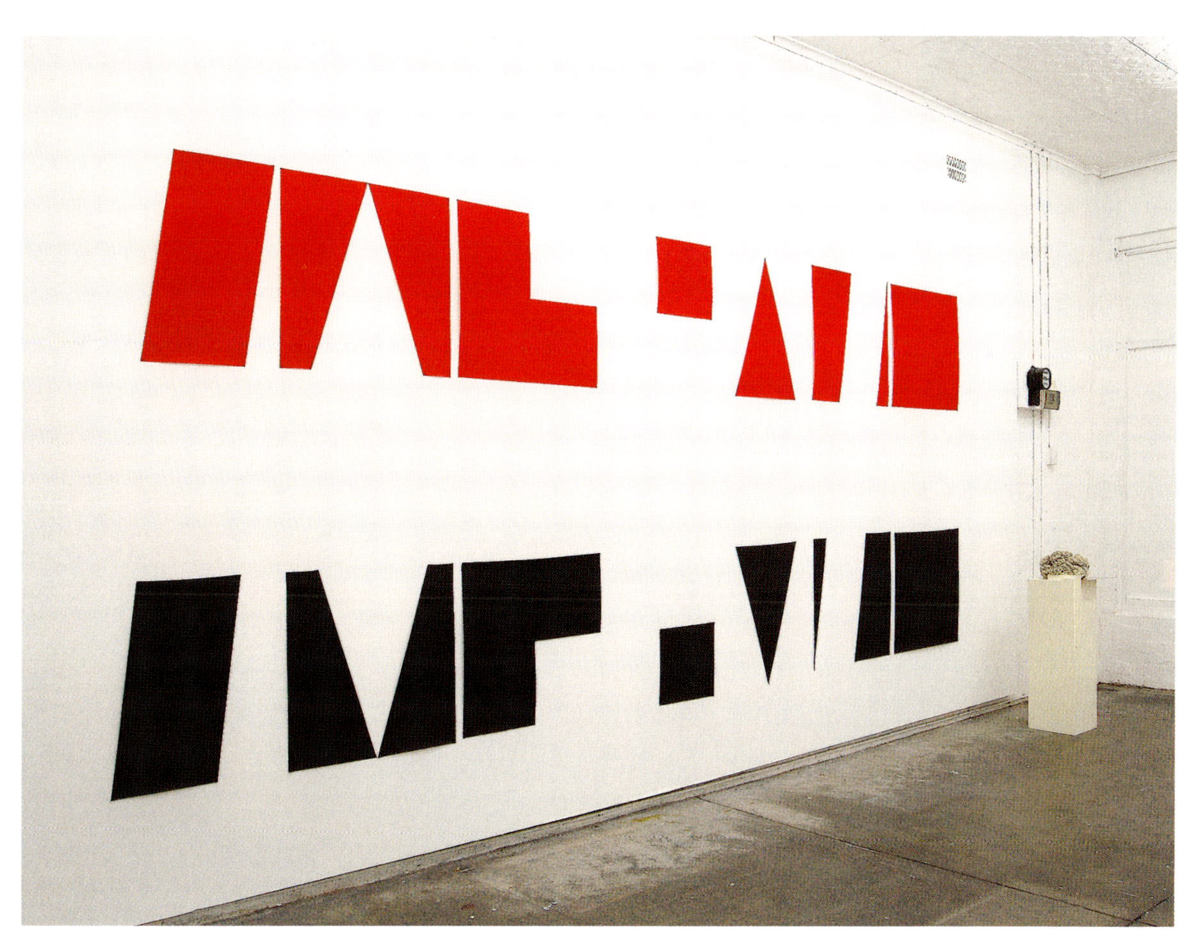

Raafat Ishak and Sean Loughrey
Fanflag 7
vinyl
2006
courtesy the artists and Sutton Gallery

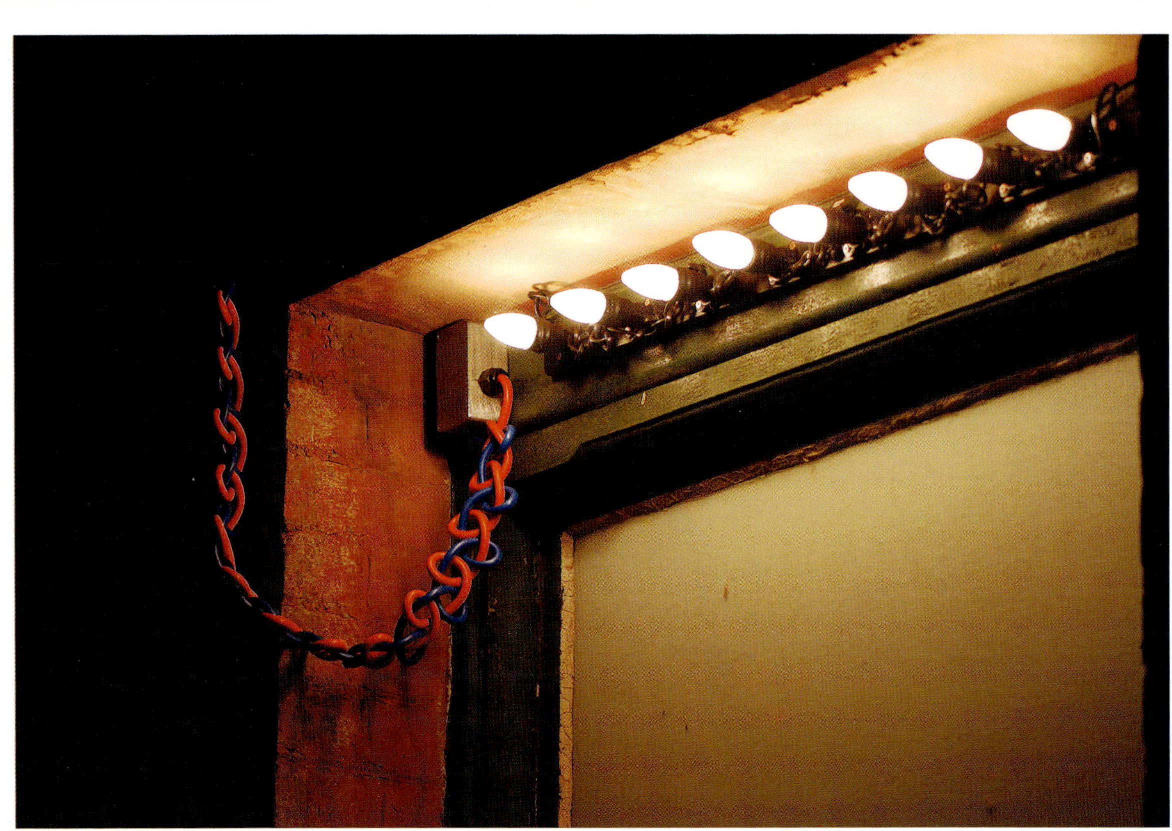

above and opposite:
Jonathan Luker
Open
electrical cord and lights
2009

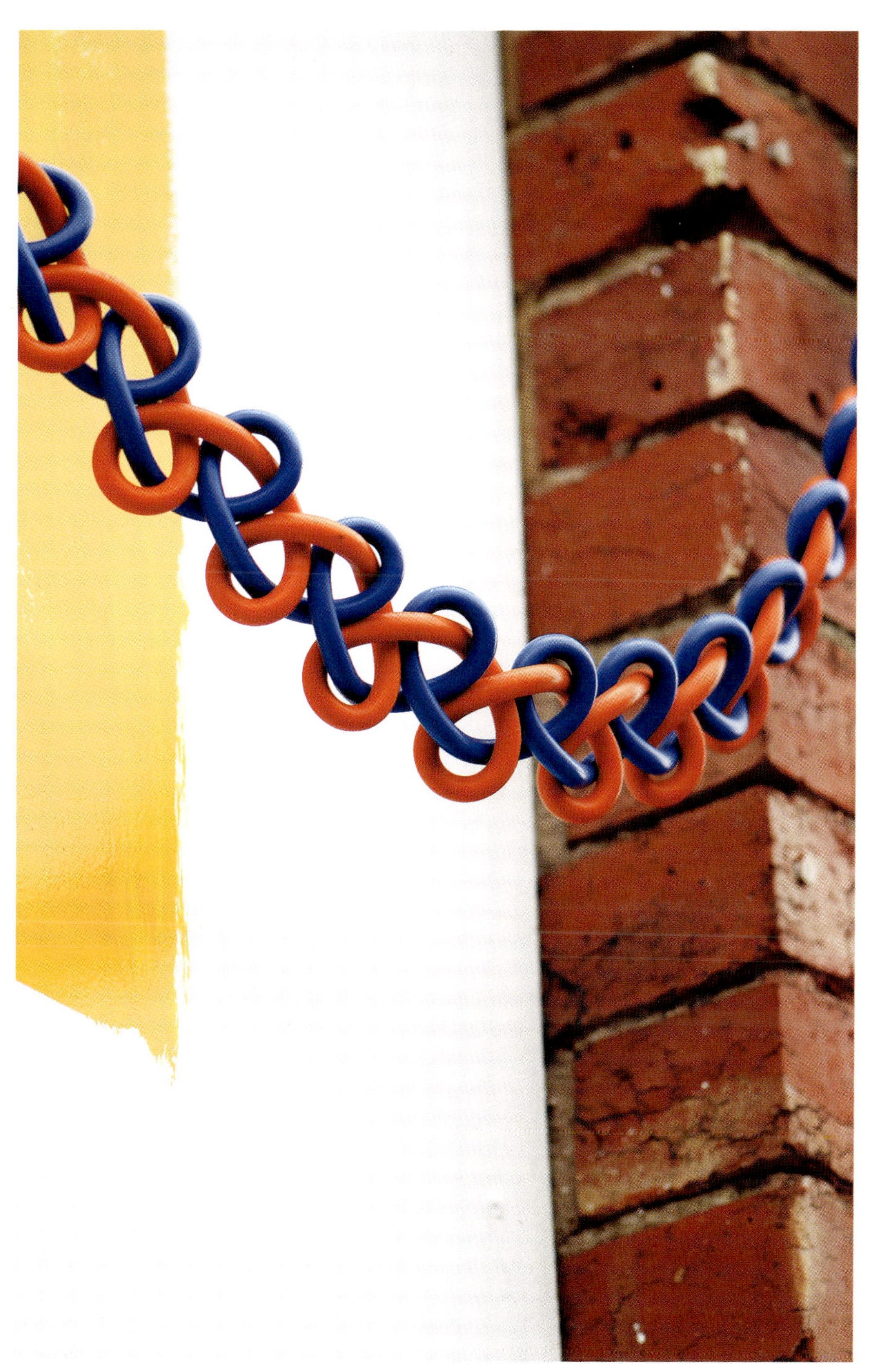

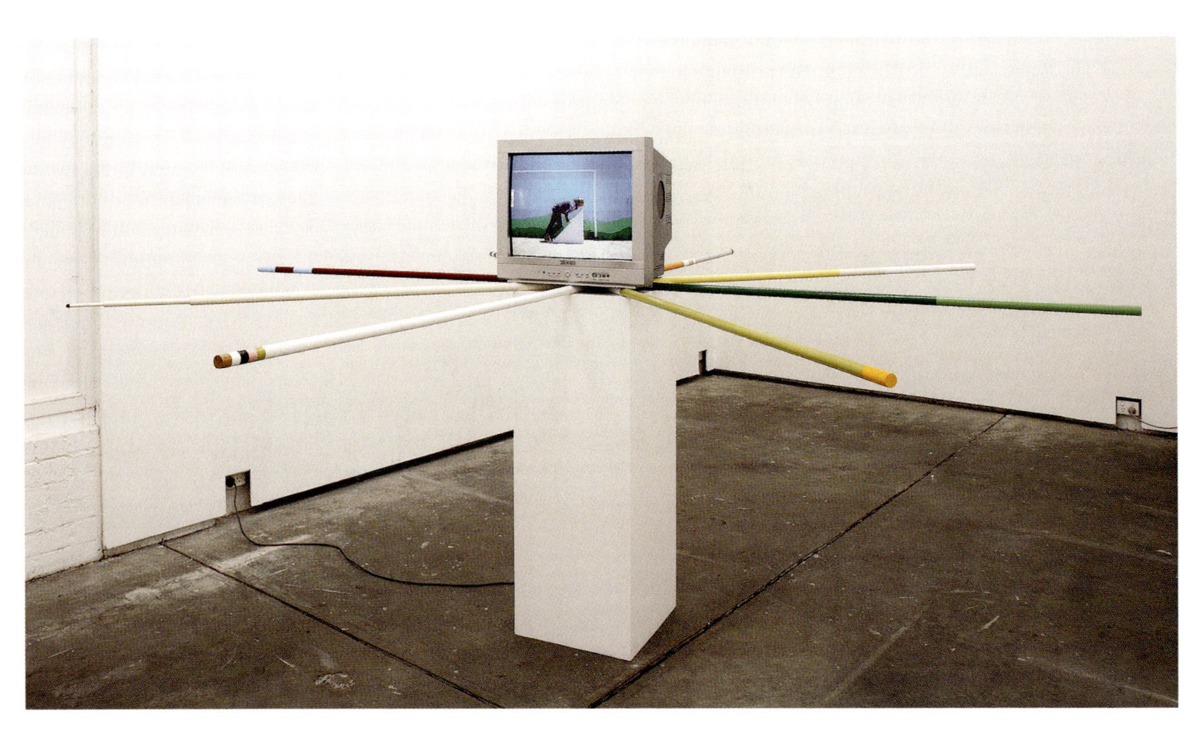

Laresa Kosloff
New Diagonal
plinth, painted dowel sticks, television monitor (video duration: 3 mins)
2007
photograph: Andrew Curtis
courtesy the artist and Anna Schwartz Gallery

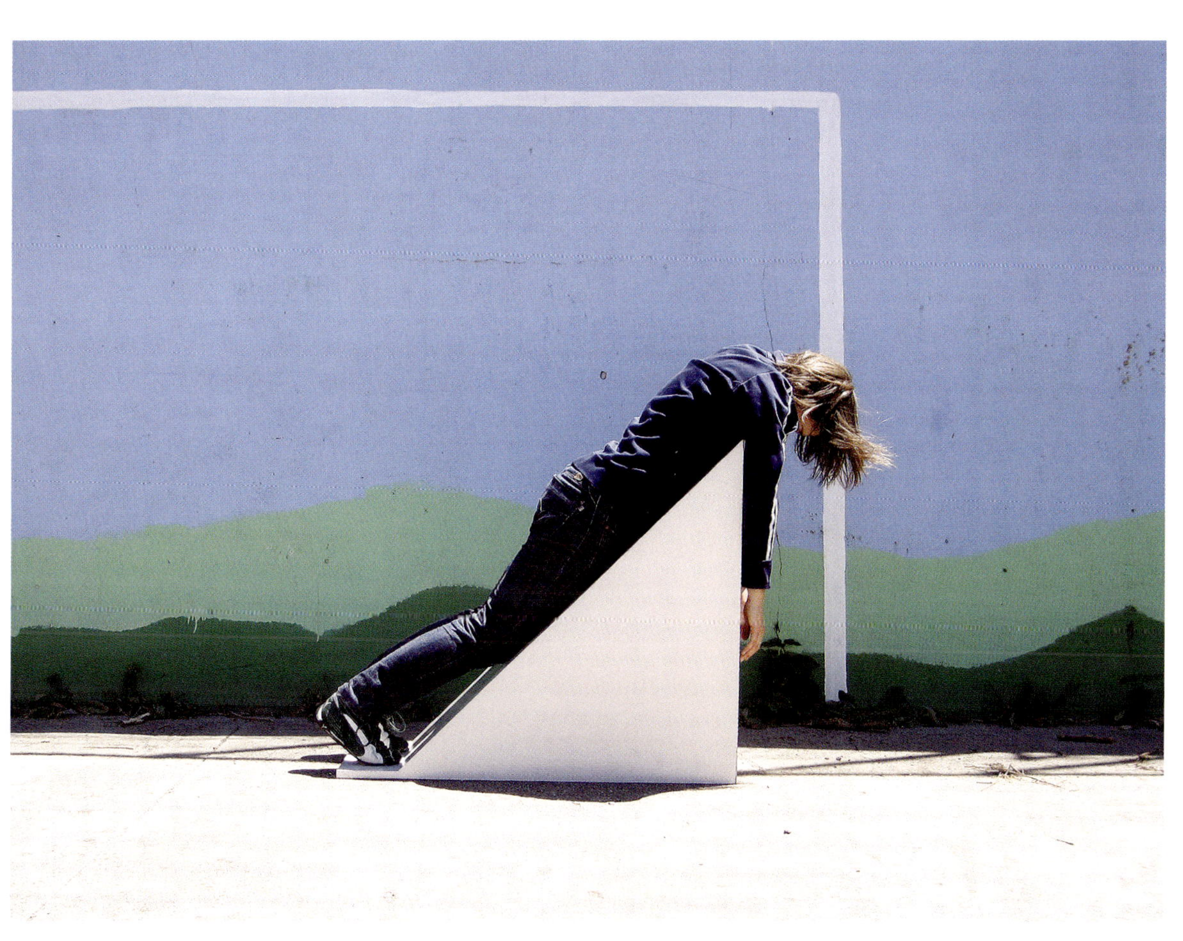

Laresa Kosloff
New Diagonal
video still (video duration: 3 mins)
2007
courtesy the artist and Anna Schwartz Gallery

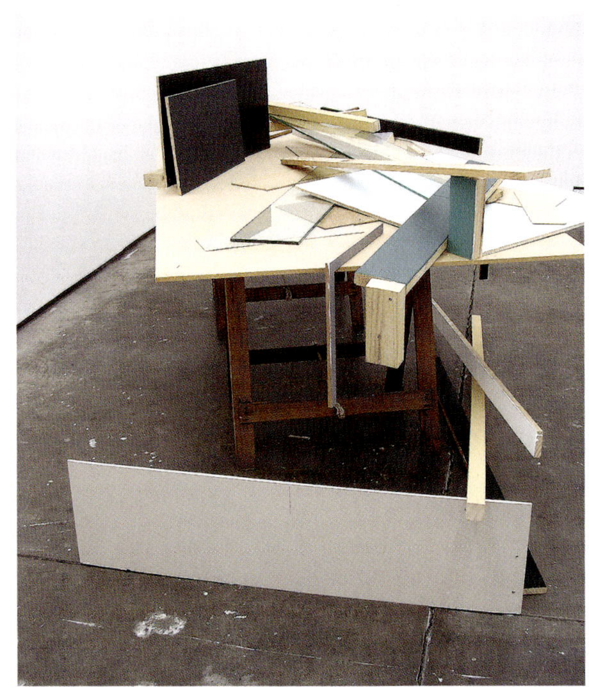

Justin Andrews, Danny Lacy, Kyle Jenkins, Masato Takasaka
Inverted Topology
collected materials
2007

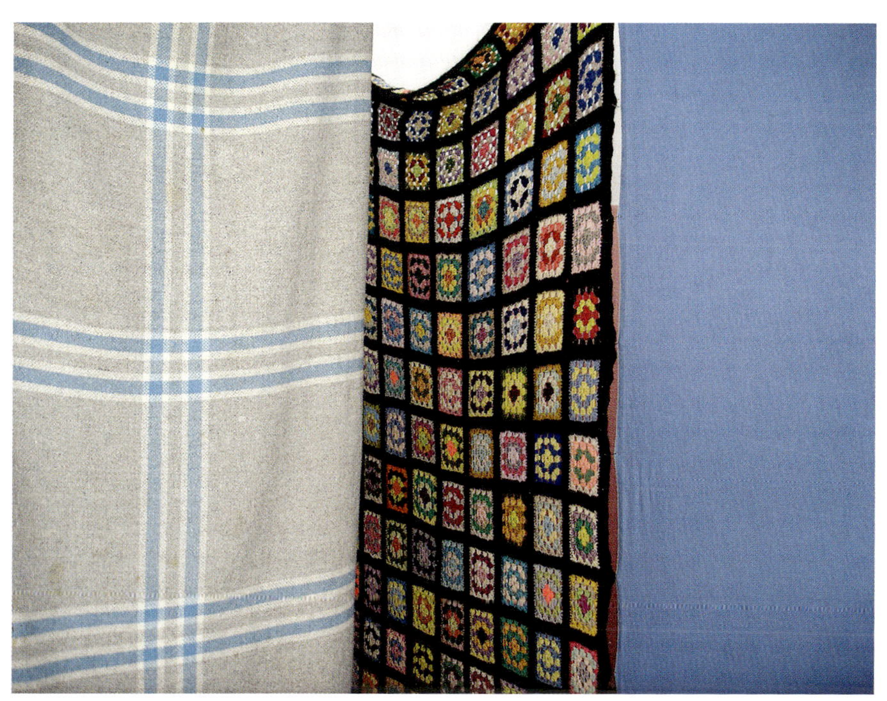

Mark McDean
my blue heaven
installation: blankets
2006

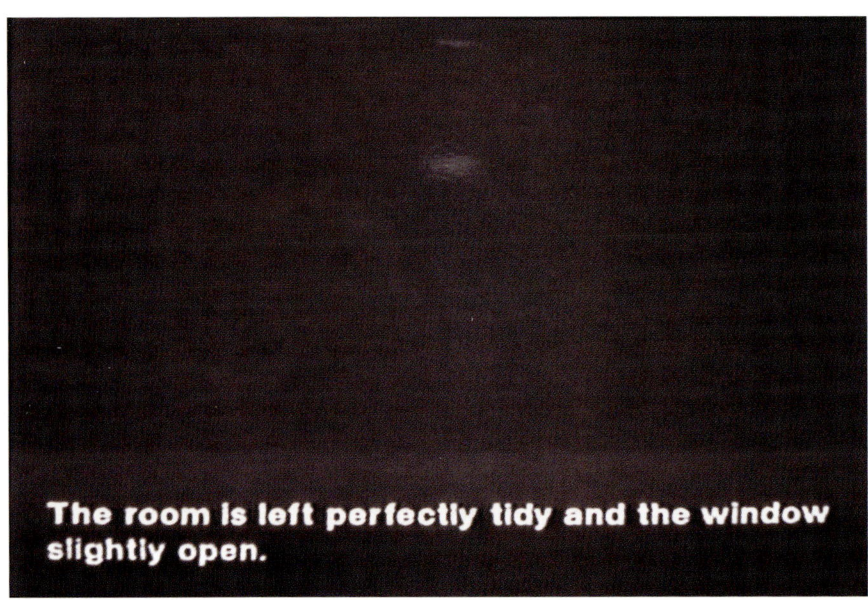

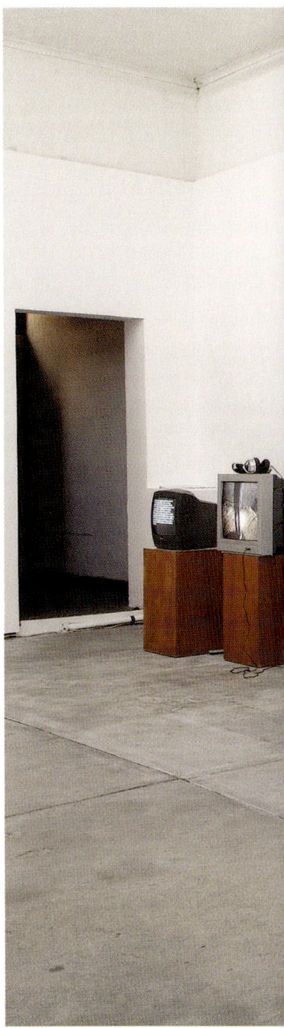

Sally Mannall
Ocular Lab Retrospective Projects #3
video still
1994–2008

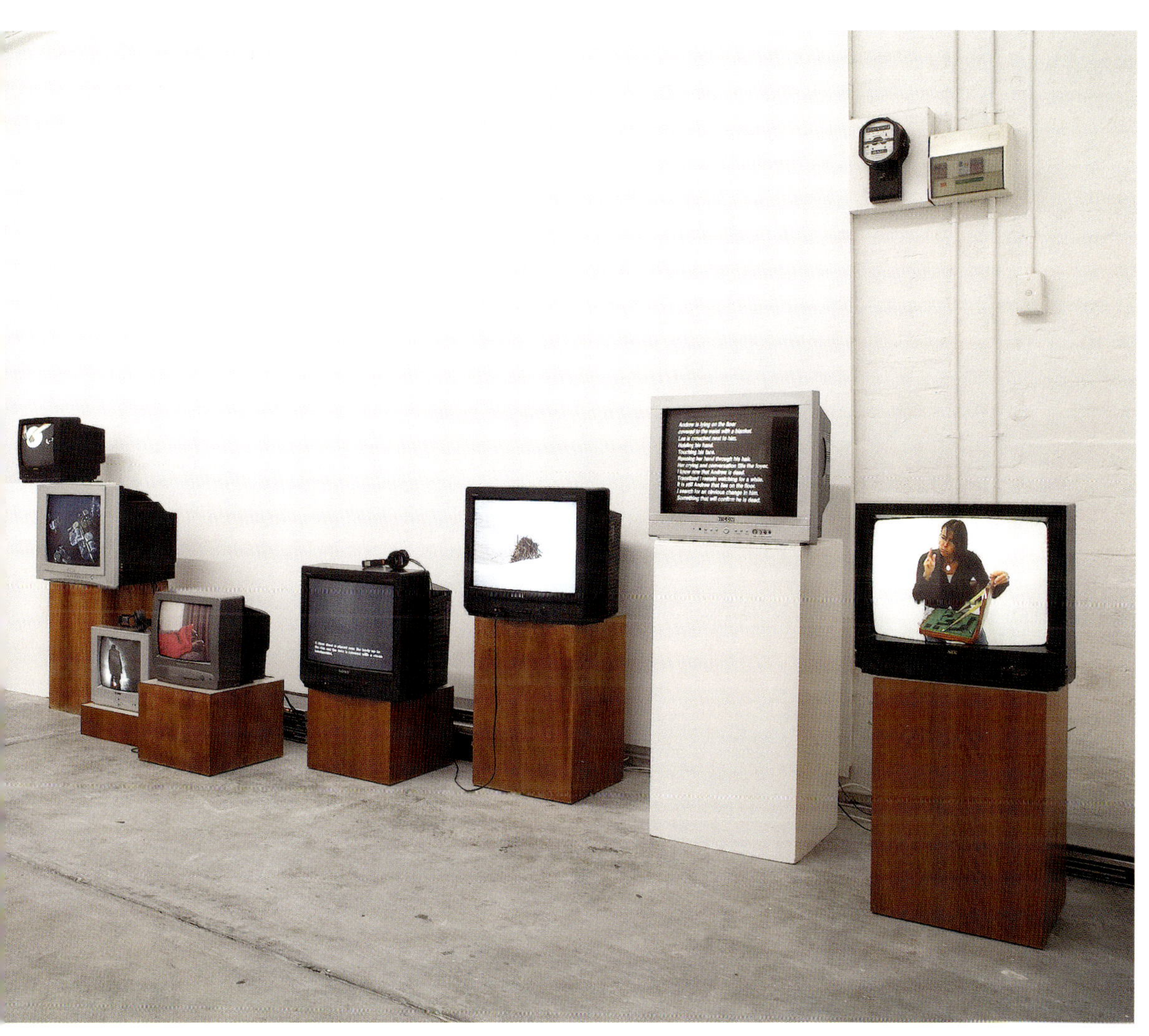

Sally Mannall
Ocular Lab Retrospective Projects #3
selected video works
1994–2008
curated by Raafat Ishak and Sandra Bridie
11 DVDs (various durations), TV monitors, DVD players, headphones, plinths
2008
photograph: Christian Capurro

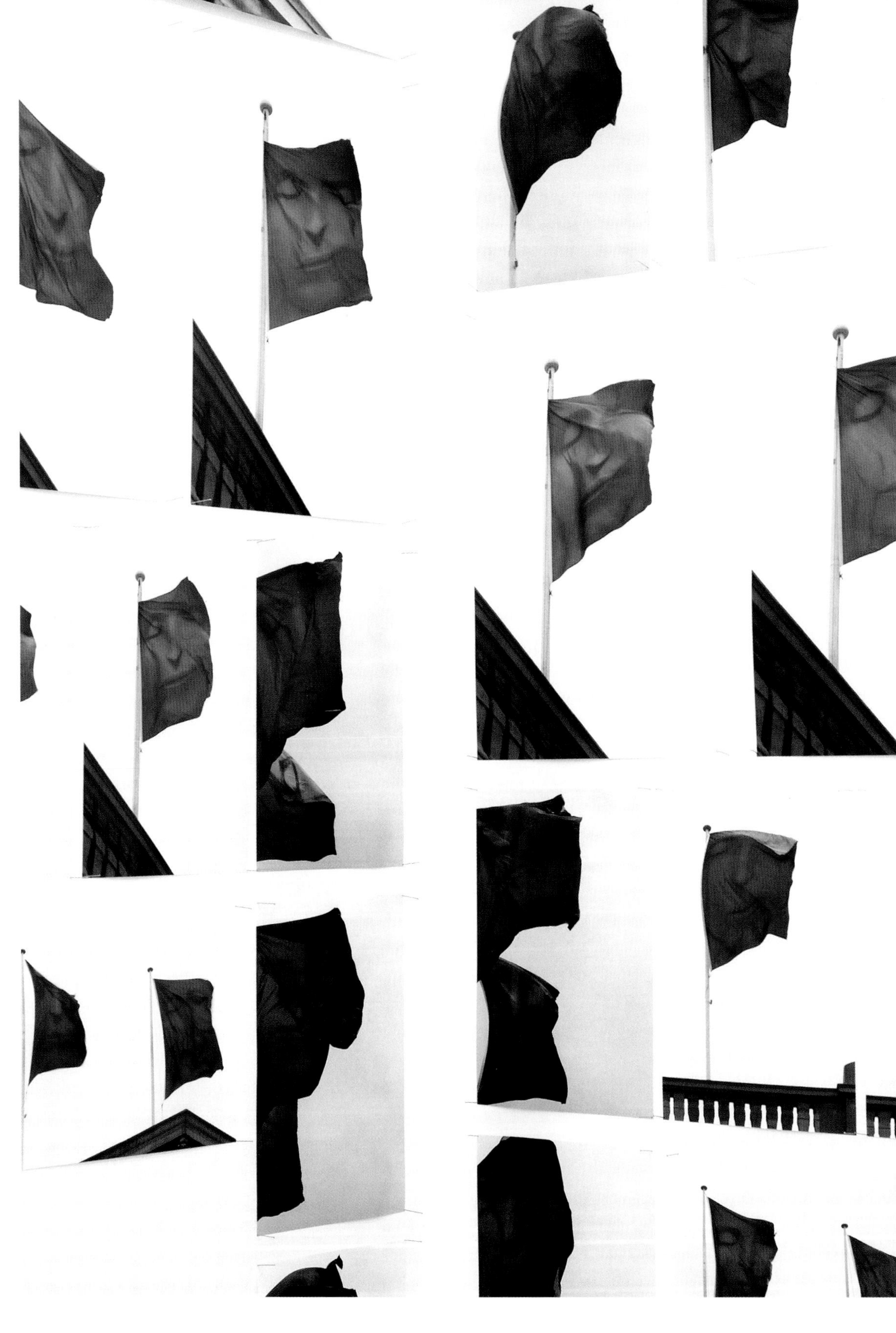

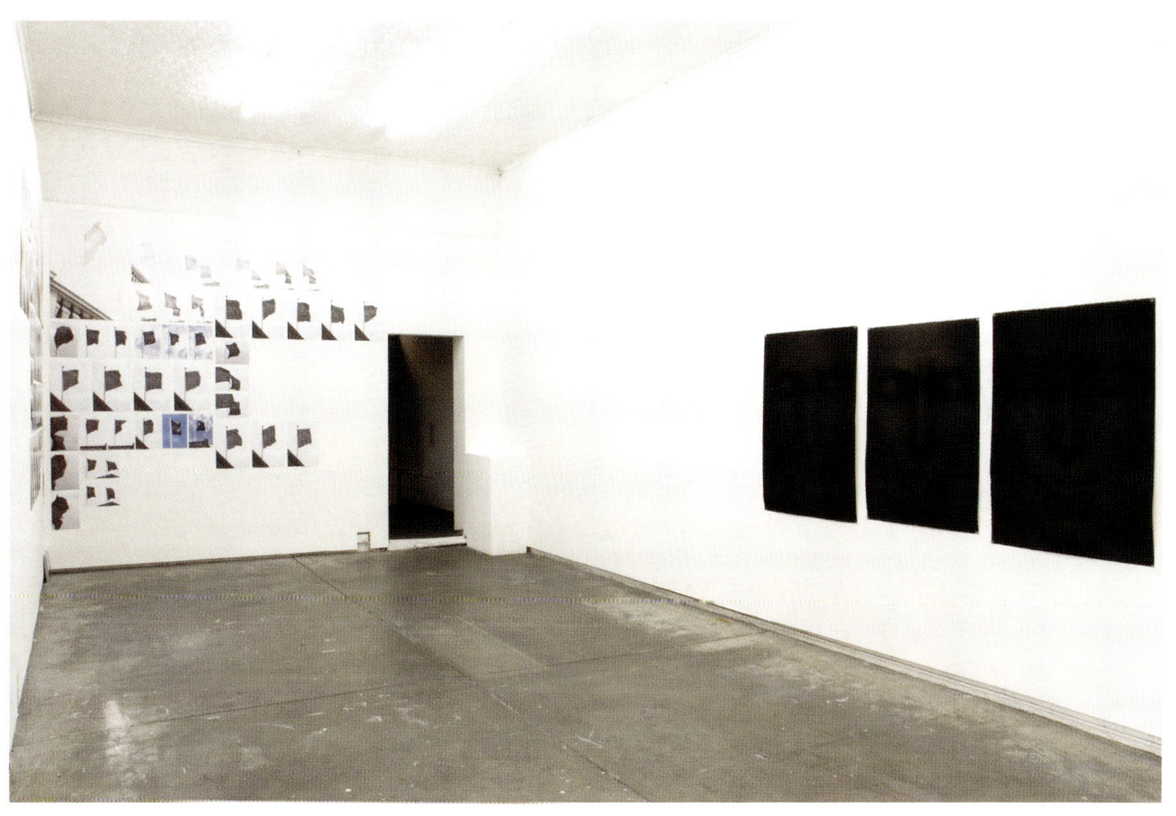

above and opposite:
Tom Nicholson
Marat at his last breath
installation views
2005–2006
three charcoal drawings, and installation of inkjet-printed photographs;
drawings each: 80 × 100cm; installation of photographs: 400 × 200cm.
This work made use of the drawings for, and photographic residues from,
Flags for a trades hall council 2005, a public installation of four flags flying
from the rooftops of Melbourne's Victorian Trades Hall Council, the peak body
for trade unions in the state of Victoria.
Marat at his last breath, a one-day exhibition held on 26 January 2006,
was conceived as a 'site-specific' installation for Australia Day / Invasion Day,
a format that was subsequently revisited in several other one-day events and
exhibitions on 26 January at Ocular Lab.
photograph: Christian Capurro
courtesy the artist and Anna Schwartz Gallery

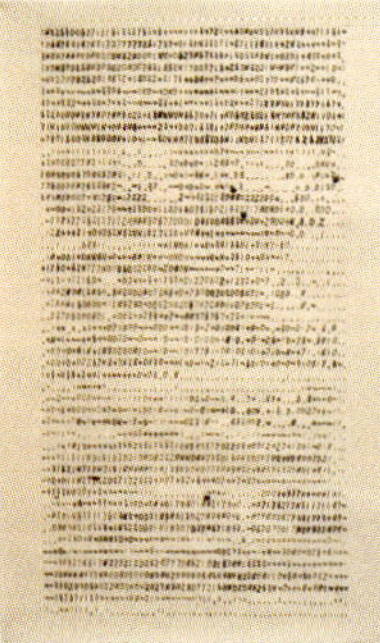
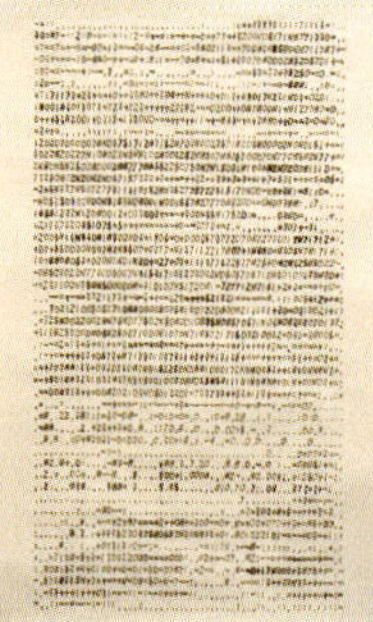
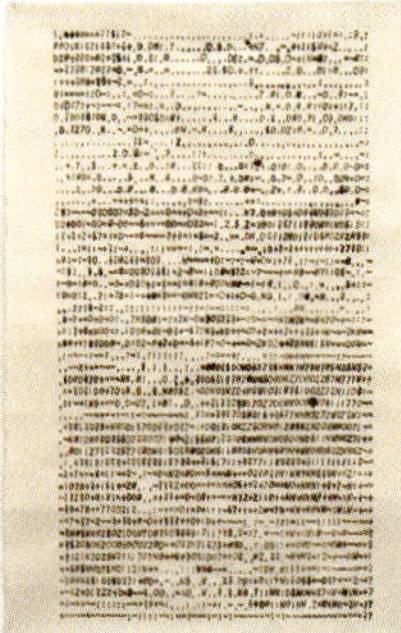
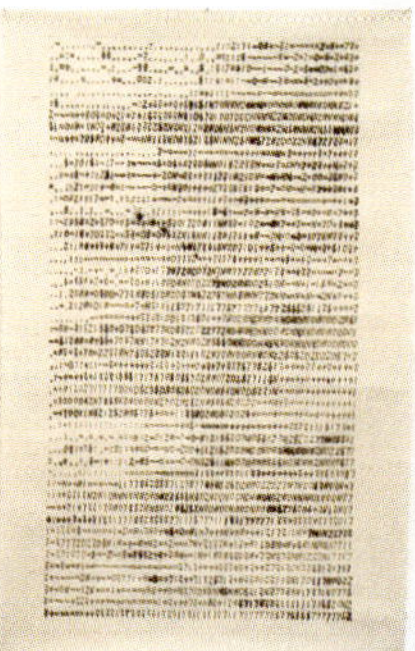

Katrin von Maltzahn (Germany)
Model drawings
pencil on paper
2007
photograph: Jan Svenungsson

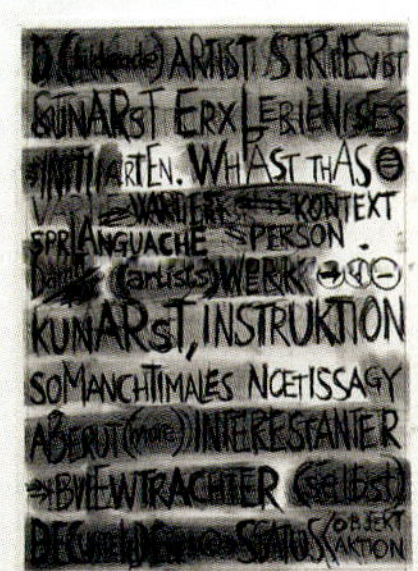

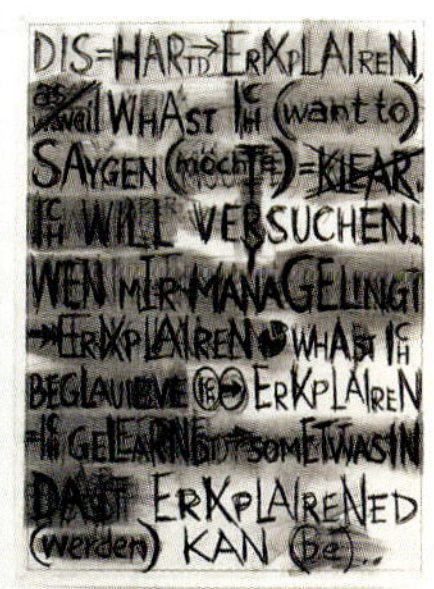

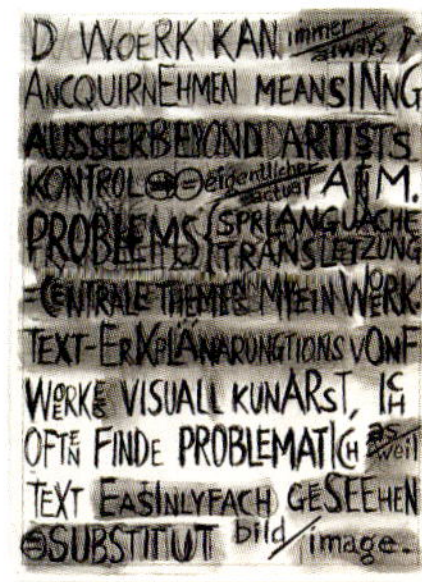

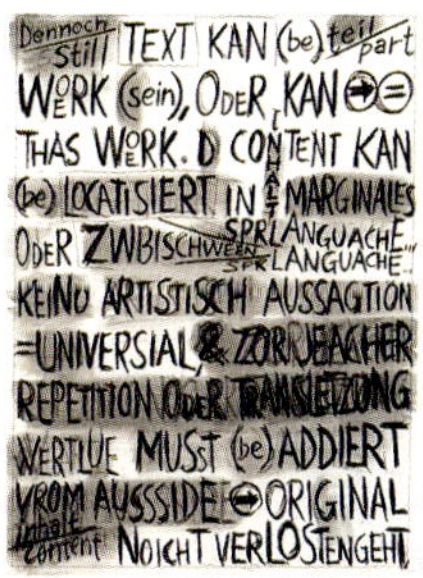

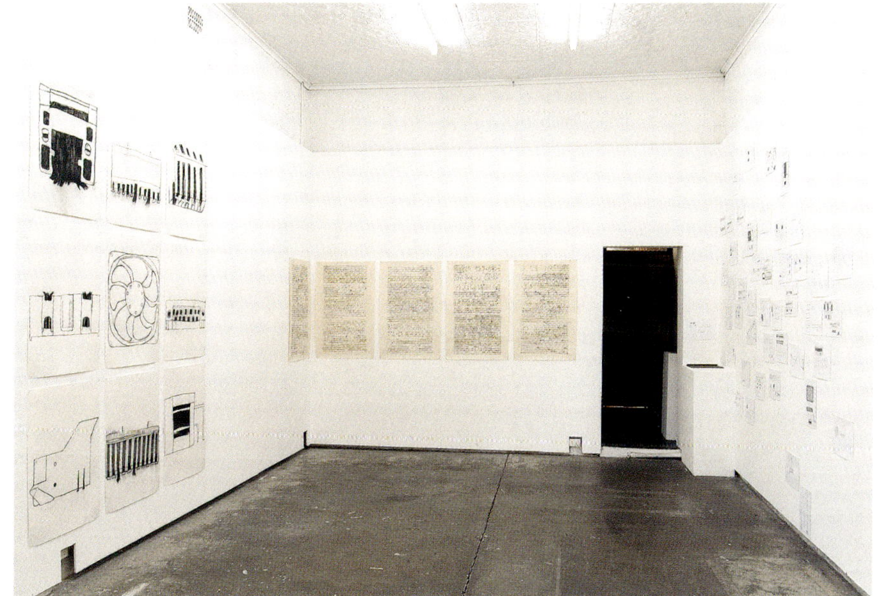

top:
Jan Svenungsson (Sweden)
Between two languages
charcoal on paper
2007
photograph: Jan Svenungsson

bottom:
Katrin von Maltzahn and Jan Svenungsson
Being the Mirror
installation view
2007
photograph: Jan Svenungsson

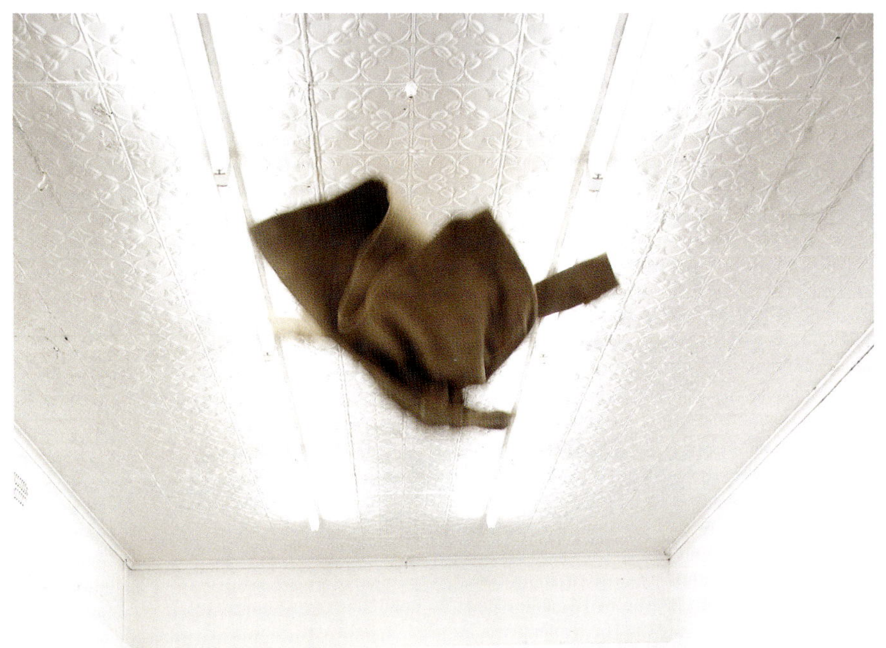

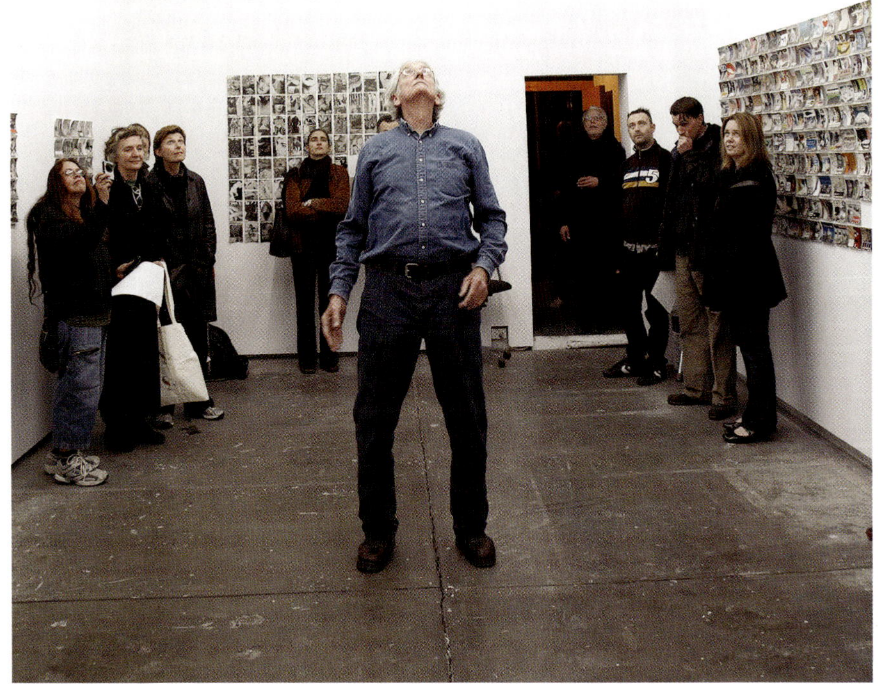

Ti Parks (UK)
Wallets etc.
performance details: duffle coat, wallets, paint tin and postcard collages
2008
photograph: Christian Capurro

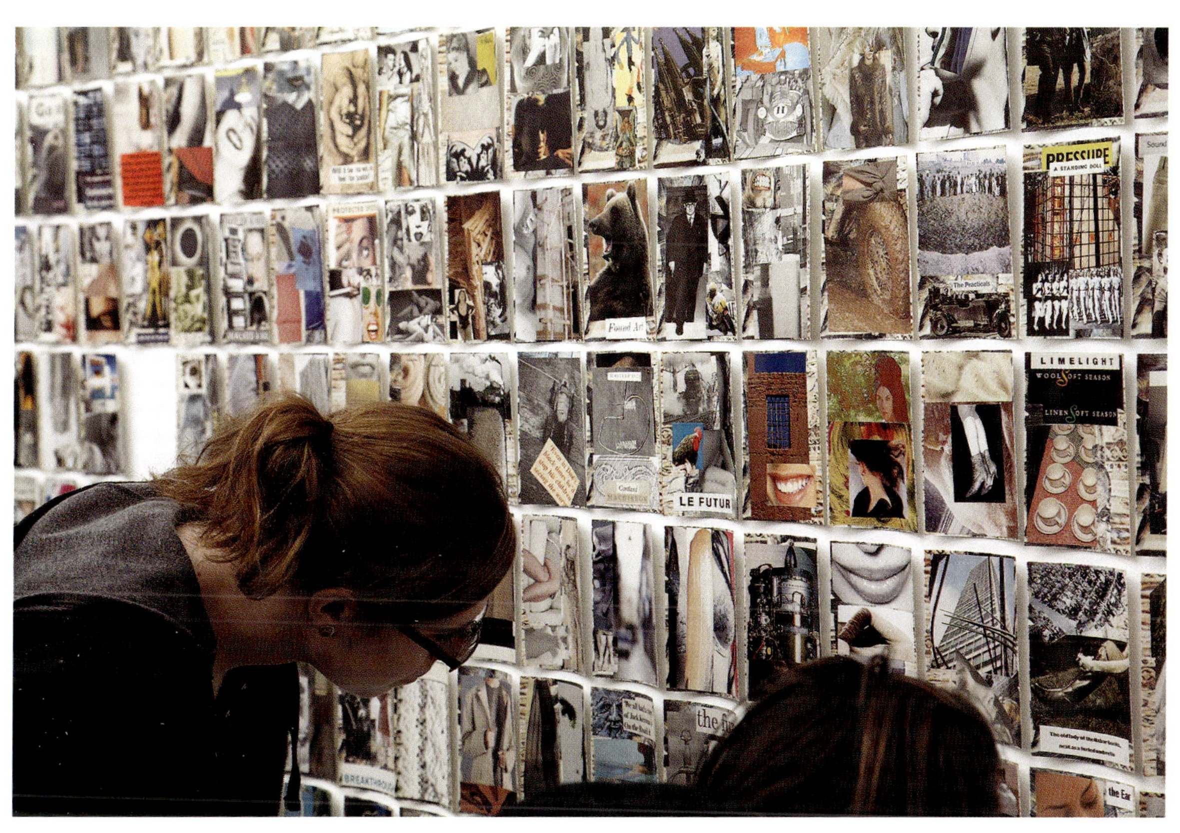

Ti Parks (UK)
A selection from the 10,000 collages
2008
photograph: Christian Capurro

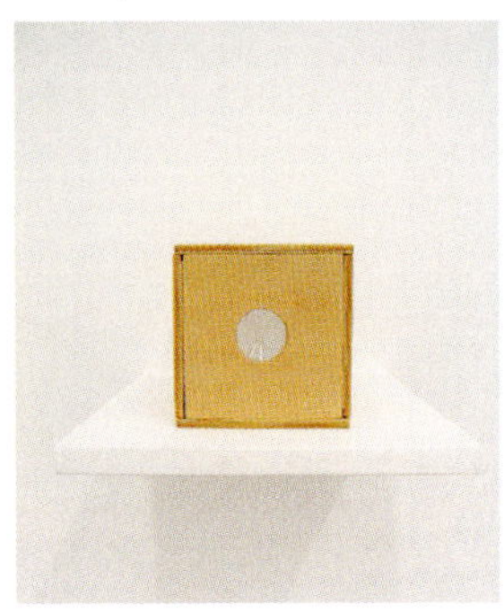

above and opposite:
Nick Devlin and Monique Ponsardin
curated by Kirsten Rann
White Cube
plaster wall, wooden box and plasticine figure
2006
courtesy the artists and Fehily Contemporary

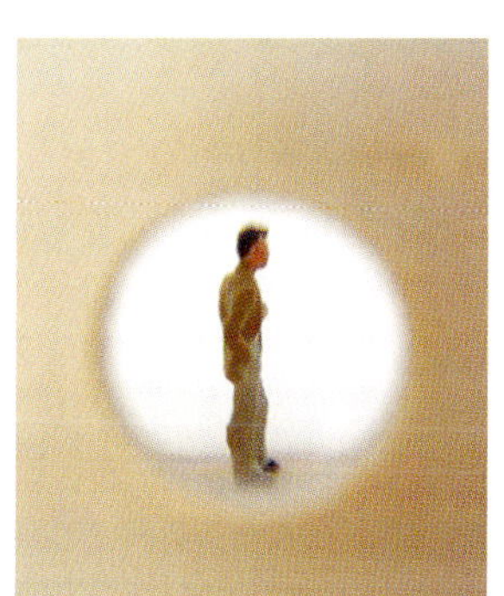

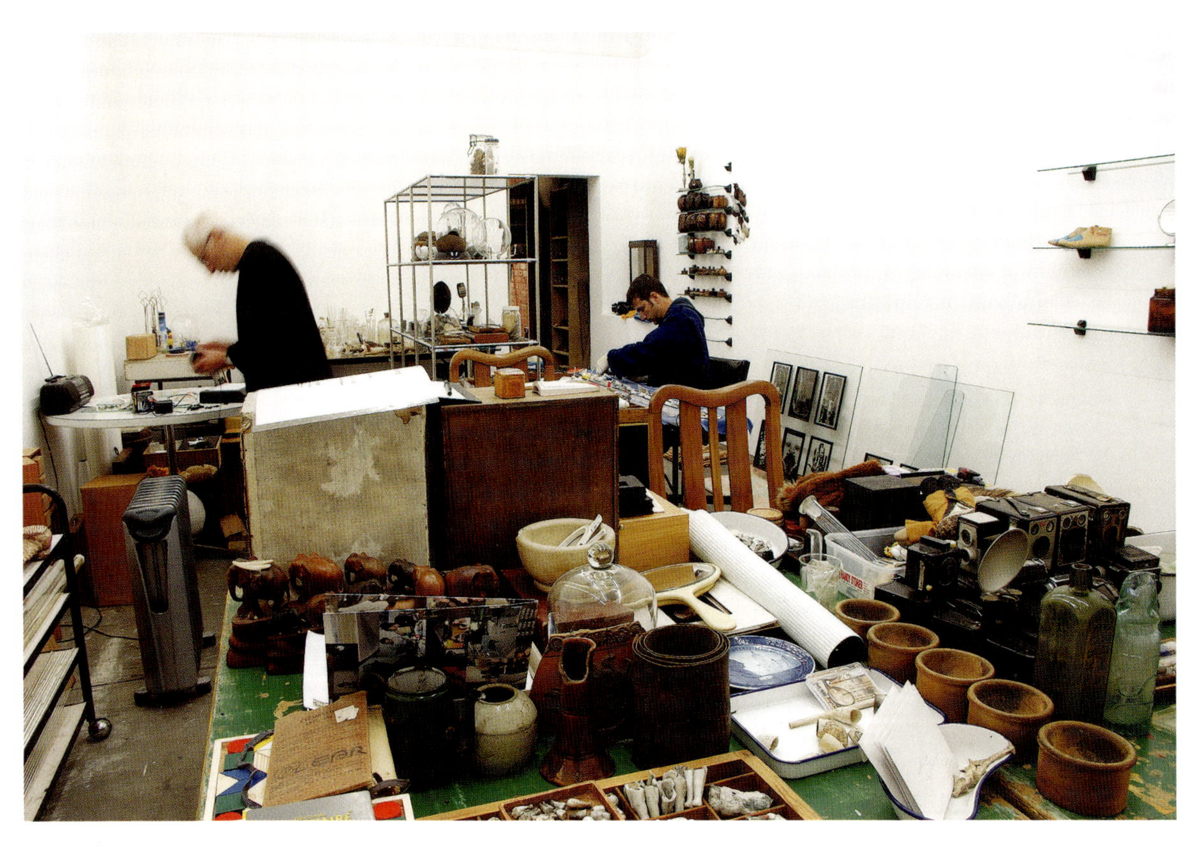

Alex Rizkalla and Victor Georgopoulos
R is for relics, remains and ruins
view of the artists installing the project
2007
courtesy the artists and Place Gallery

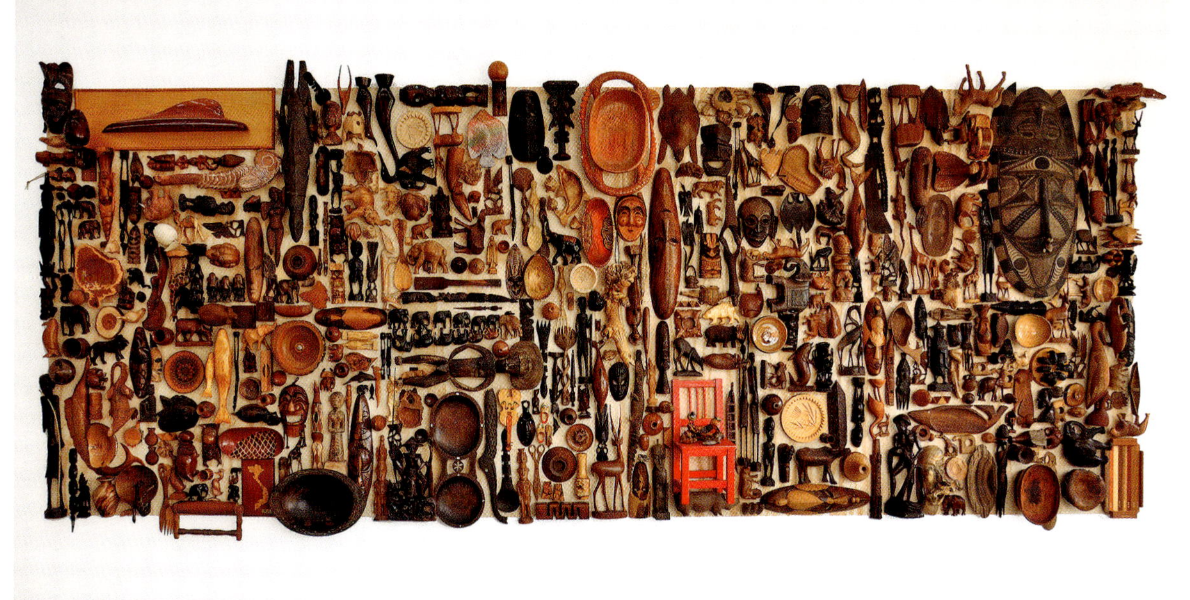

Alex Rizkalla
Deadwood
wooden objects retrieved from opportunity shops
2010
courtesy the artist and Place Gallery

opposite:
Alex Rizkalla
Memento Horribilis: W is for walking stick, war and witness
walking sticks, glow-in-the-dark paint and stainless steel rail
2004
courtesy the artist and Place Gallery

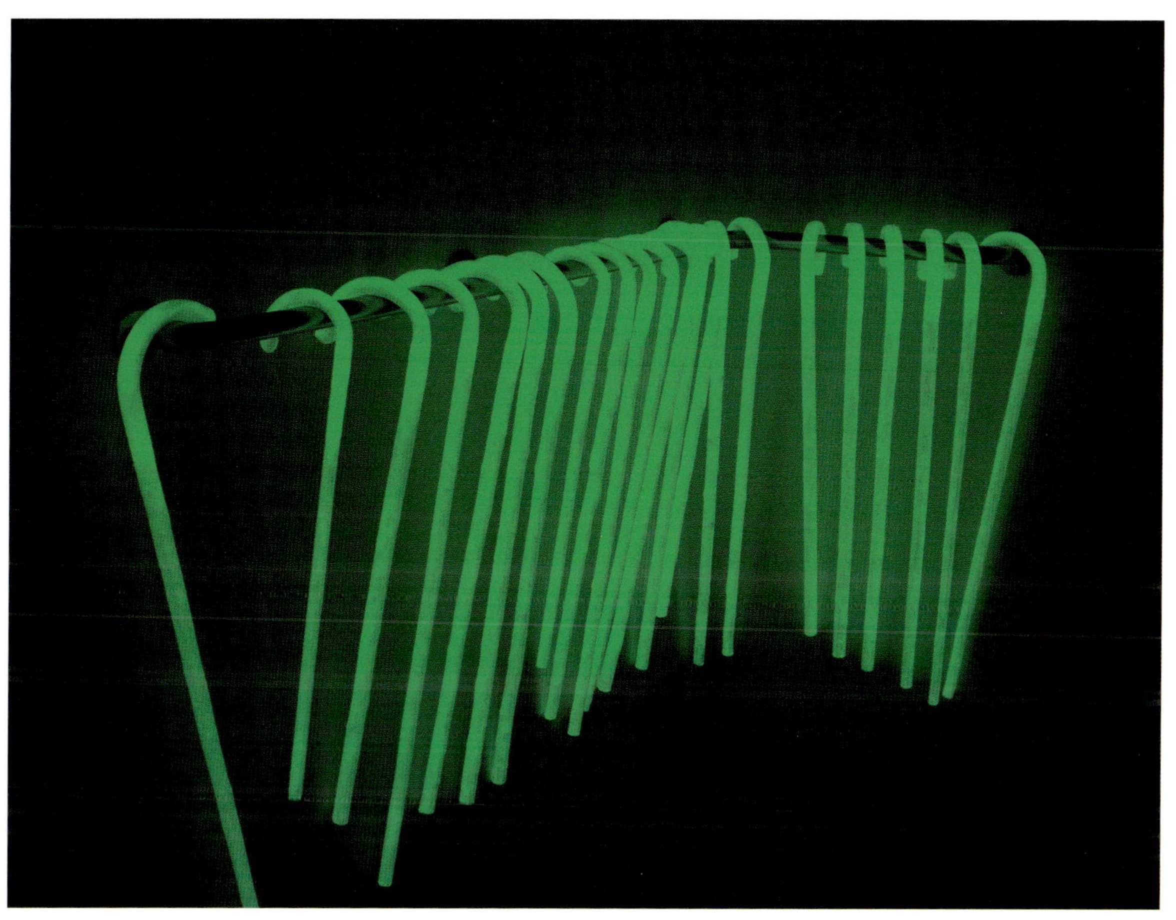

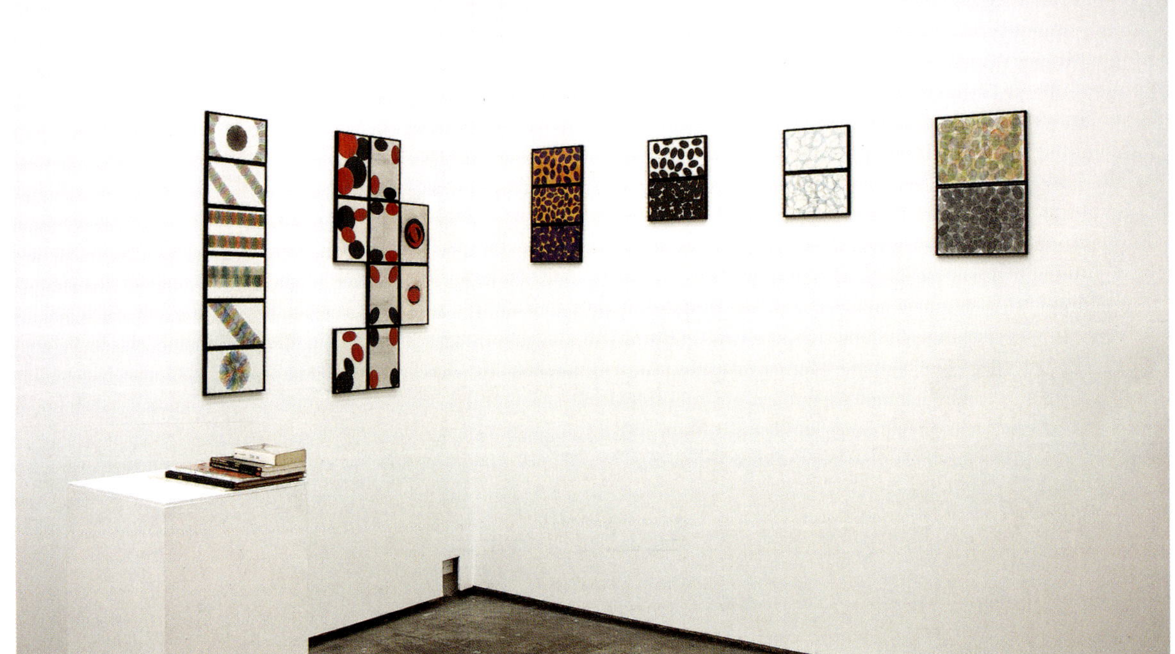

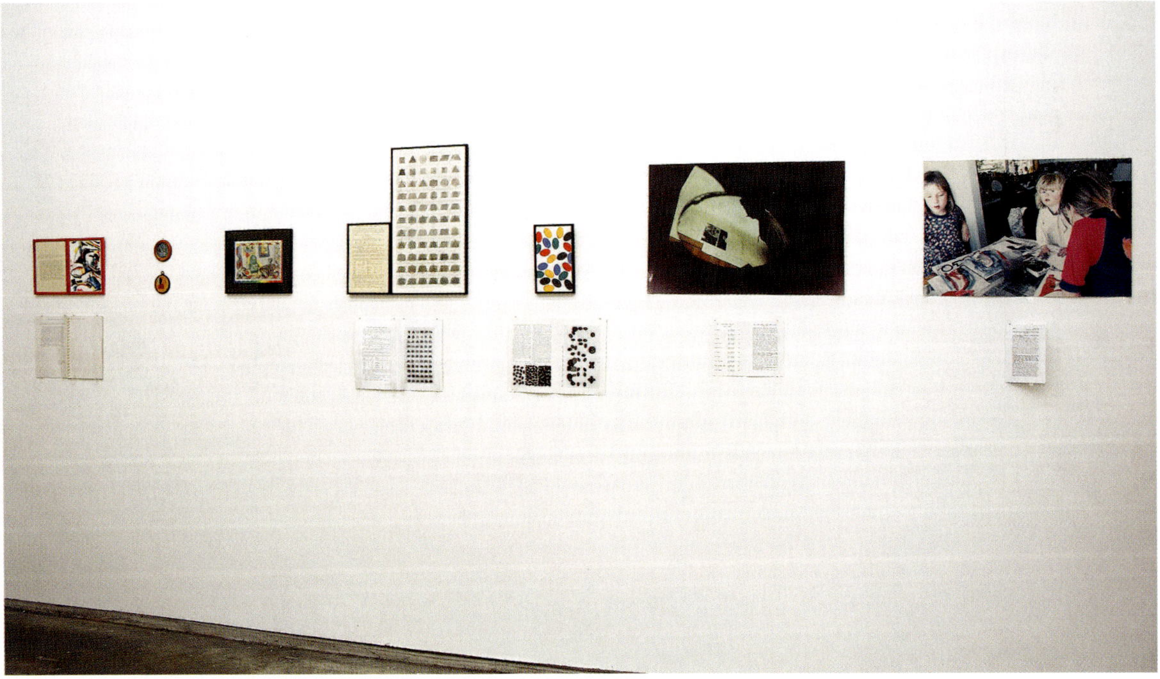

above and opposite:
Sandra Bridie
Ocular Lab Retrospective Projects #1: Sandra Bridie
installation of Jane Bridie's collection of SB works with accompanying text (detail)
various media, dimensions variable
2007

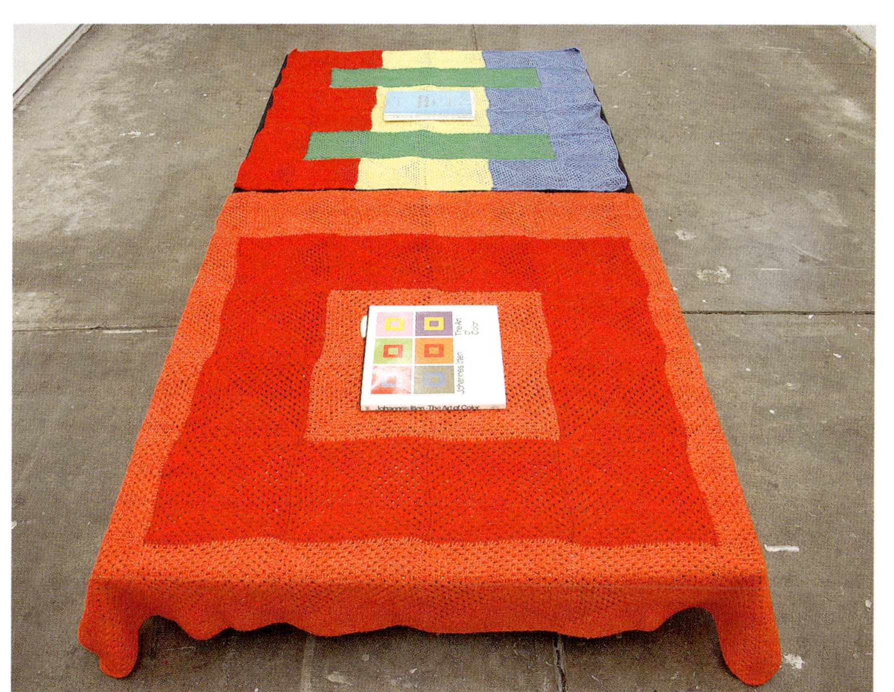
The Art of Color
Johannes Itten
Johannes Itten · The Art of Color

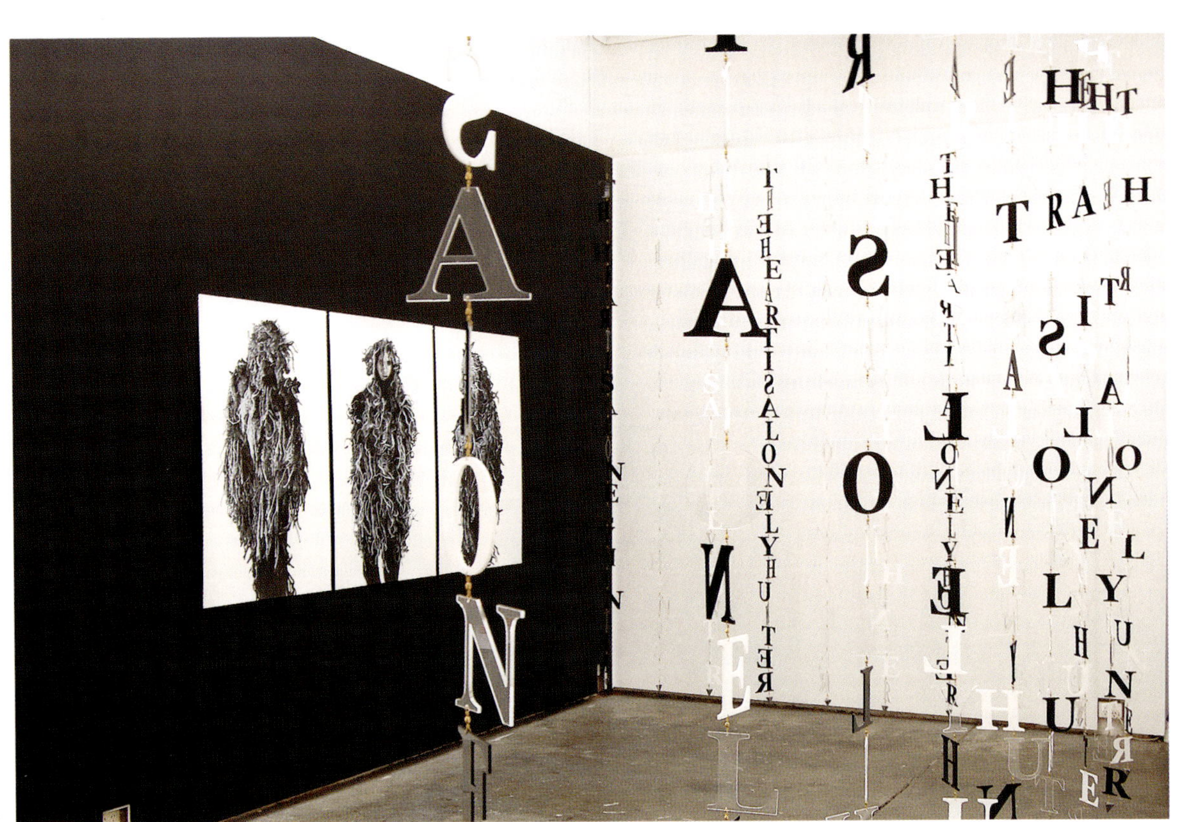

Neil Emmerson
Wood nymph triptych (the heart is a lonely hunter)
wood block print and acrylic laser-cut text
2006

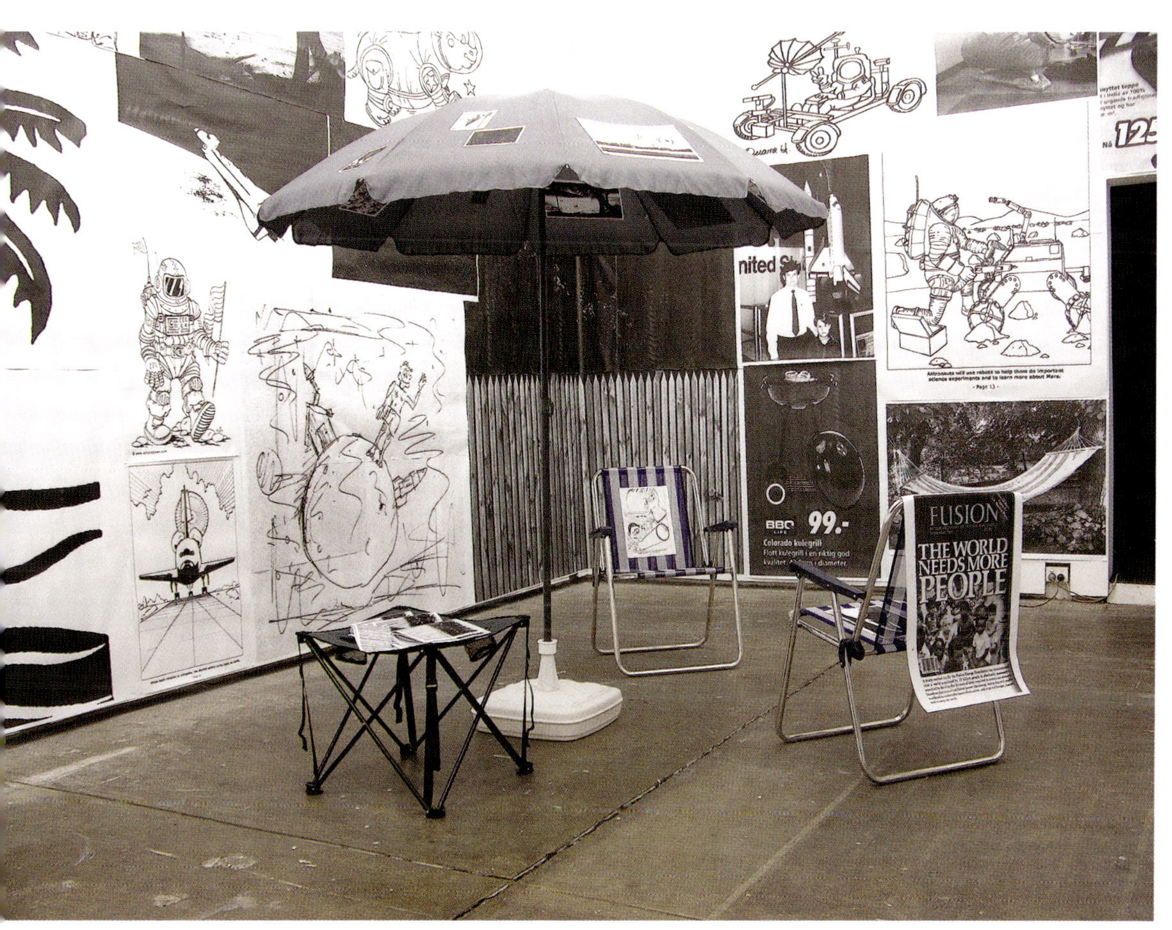

Kalle Runeson (Sweden)
hosted by Nick Mangan
Fictonalizing Philosophers Comfort Zone
installation: photocopies, beach furniture
2006
photograph: Kalle Runeson

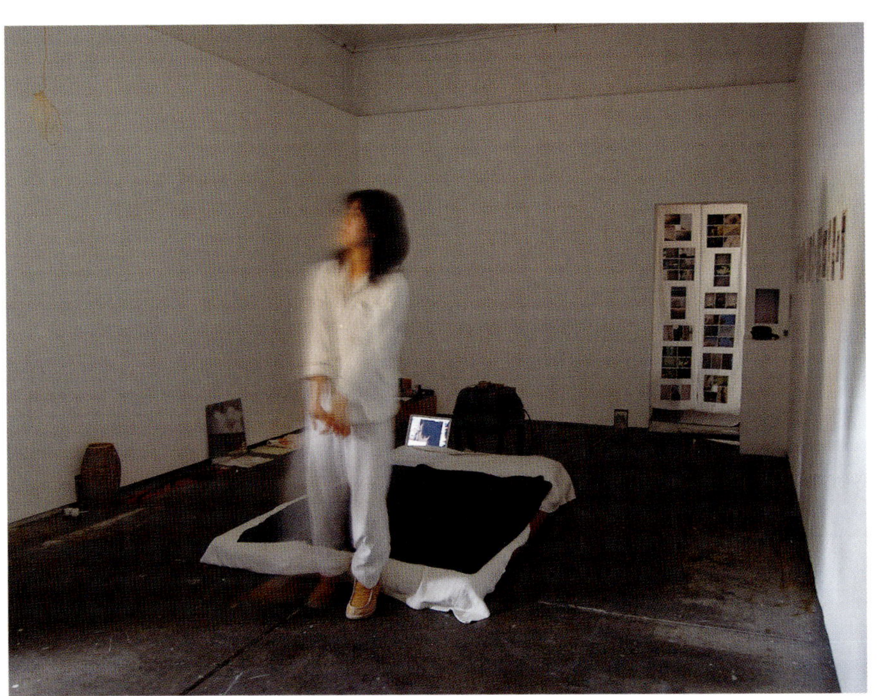

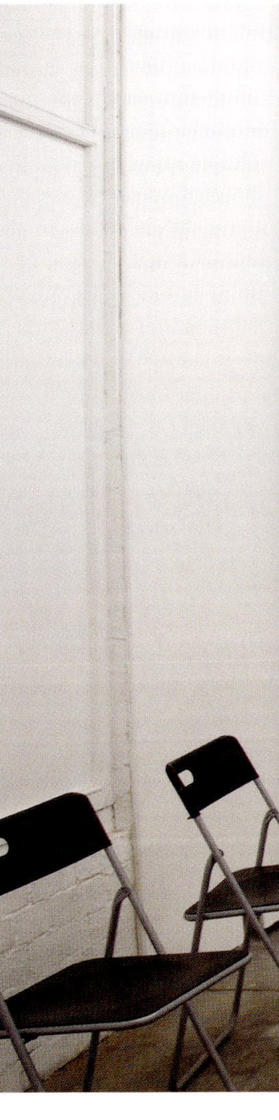

Utako Shindo
The Pro(d)a(u)ct of Love
performance detail
2006

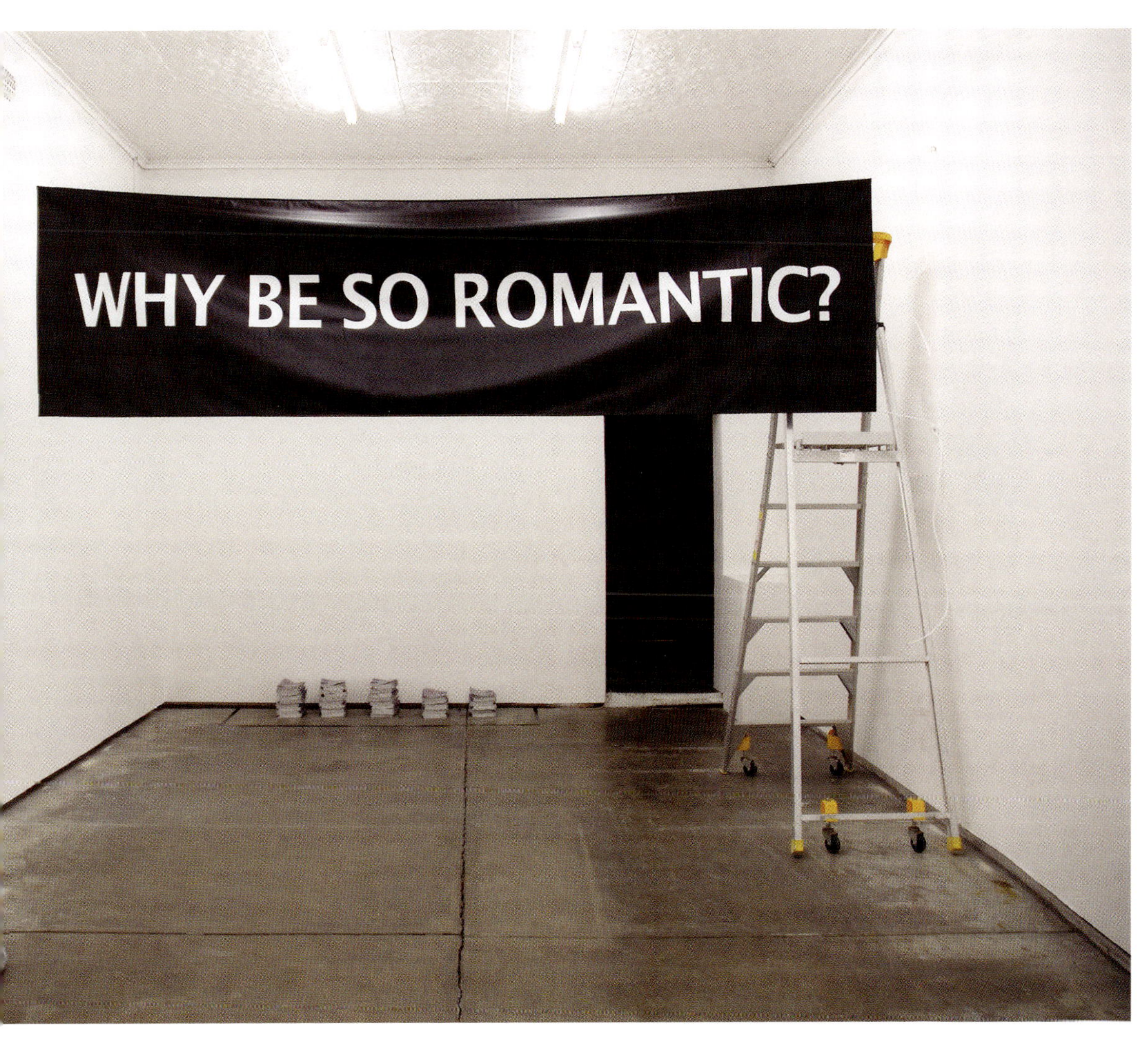

Fiona Macdonald
GENERA
installation: *Why be so romantic?*, banner, vinyl and rope; *Gratuitous Intent*, stack, 24-page book and black tape; two chairs, flourescent lights and ladder
2008

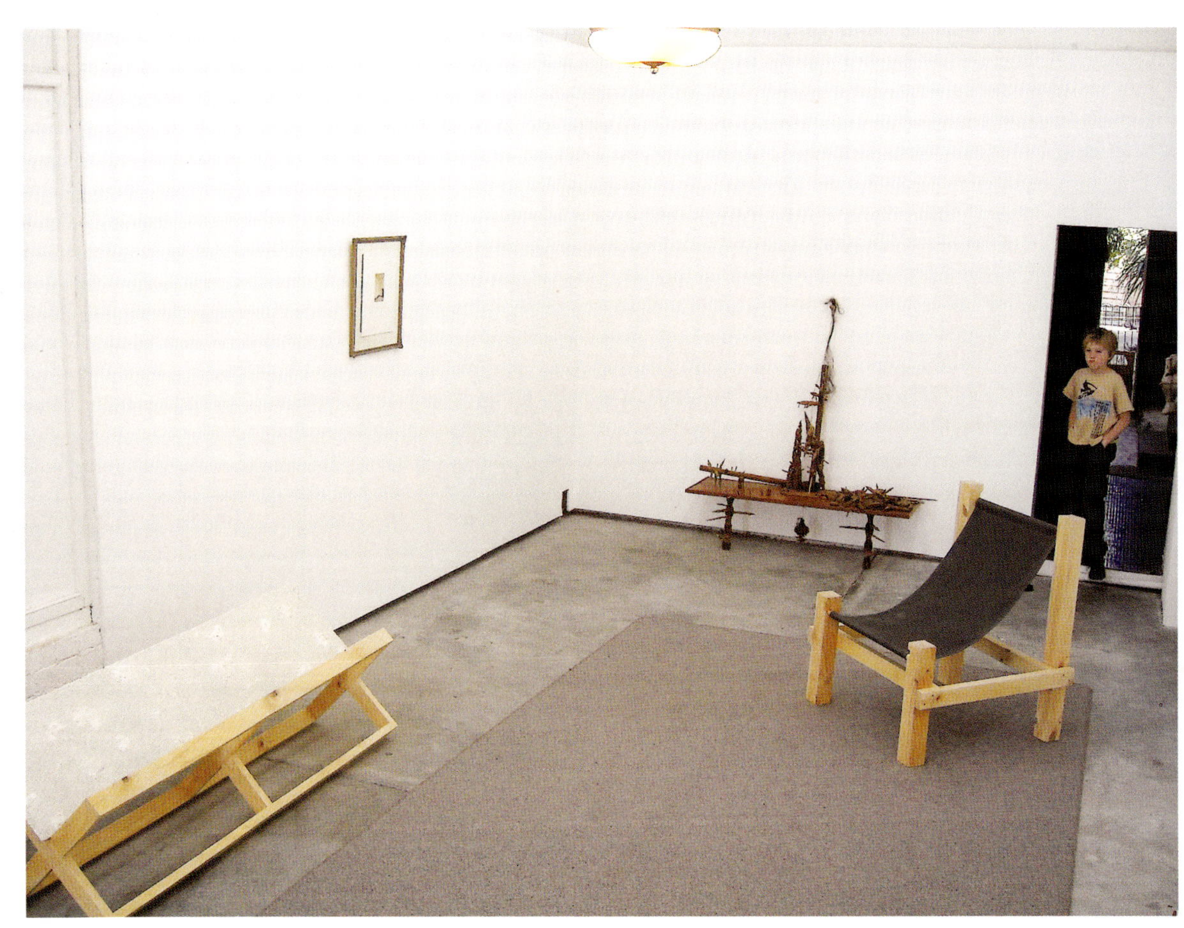

west Brunswick Sculpture Triennial (one of five sites)
organised by OSW (Terri Bird, Bianca Hester and Scott Mitchell)
including work by Fiona Abicare, Terri Bird, Stephan Bram, Nick Mangan,
Sally Marsland and Spiros Panigirakis
2009

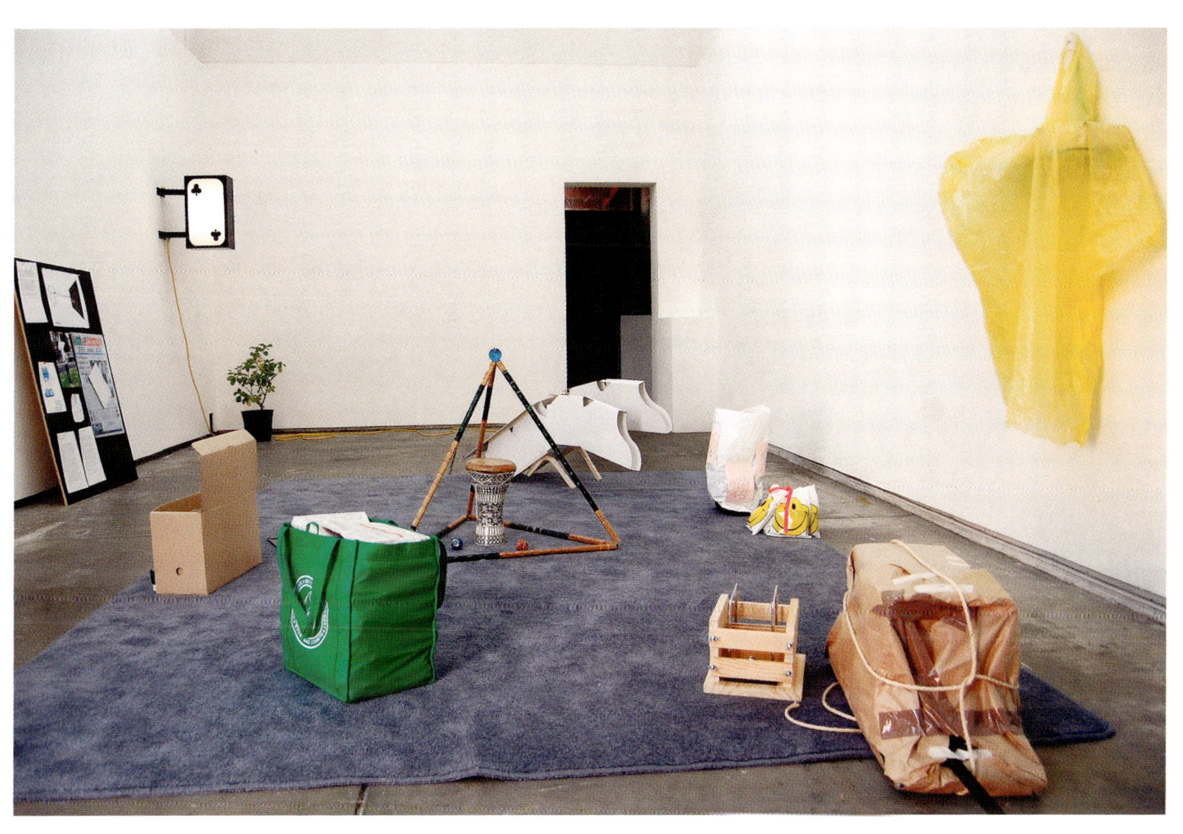

CLUBS HOSTED BY; (and hosting) OCULAR LAB
A letter sent to Ocular Lab committee:
... We hope you are interested in this proposal and look forward to hearing your response and questions. If you can determine the piece that you would like packaged, re-sited and documented in the next two weeks — we will then be able to contact you individually to arrange a time to pick up the work.
Yours sincerely, CLUBSproject Inc. with James Deutsher, Alicia Frankovich, Helen Johnson and sound padding by Castle Mice

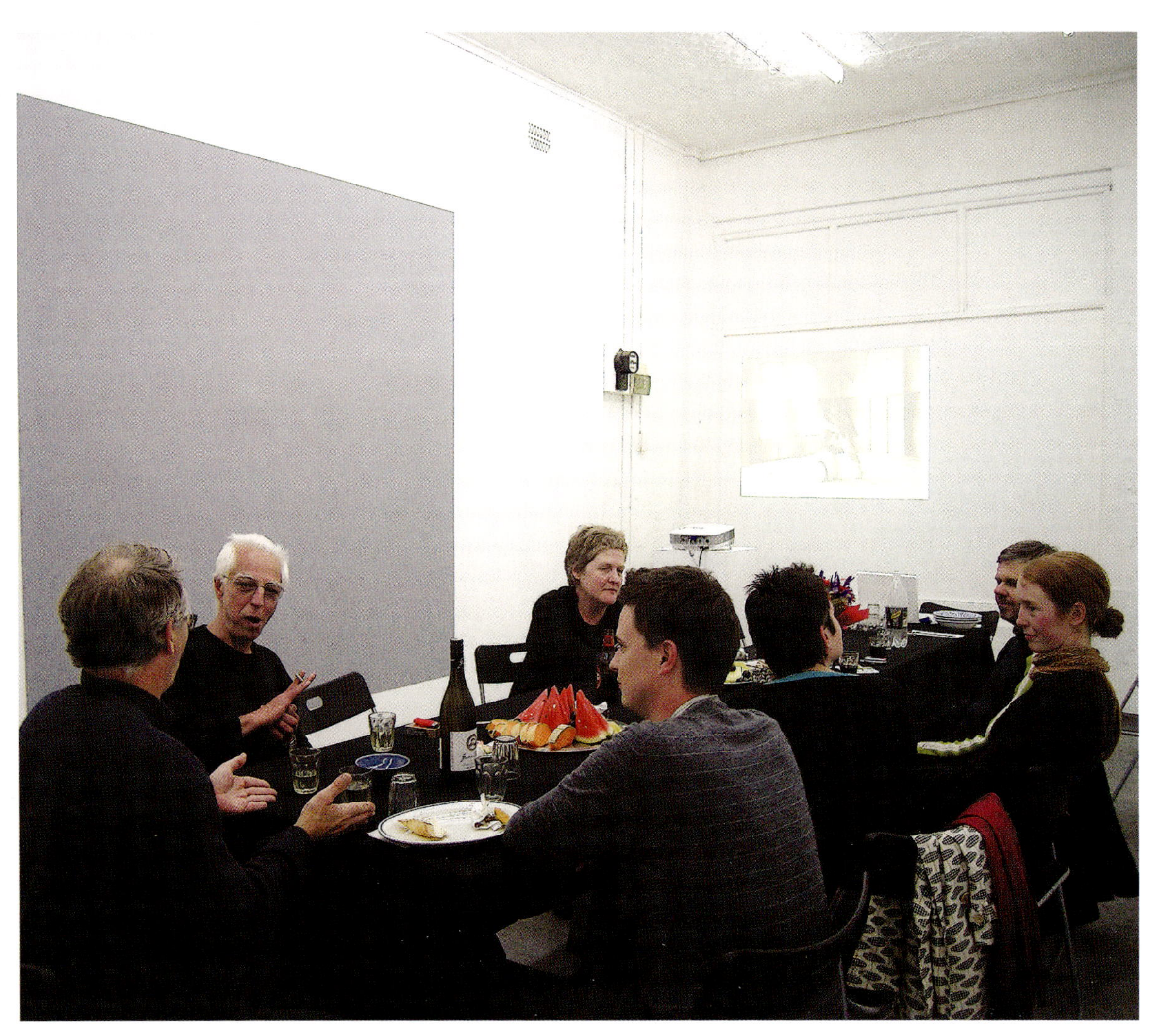

Hosting dinners at Ocular Lab Inc.
above: Ian Whittlesea (UK), 2008
opposite top: Călin Dan (Romania), 2006
opposite bottom: Kalle Ruseson (Sweden), 2006

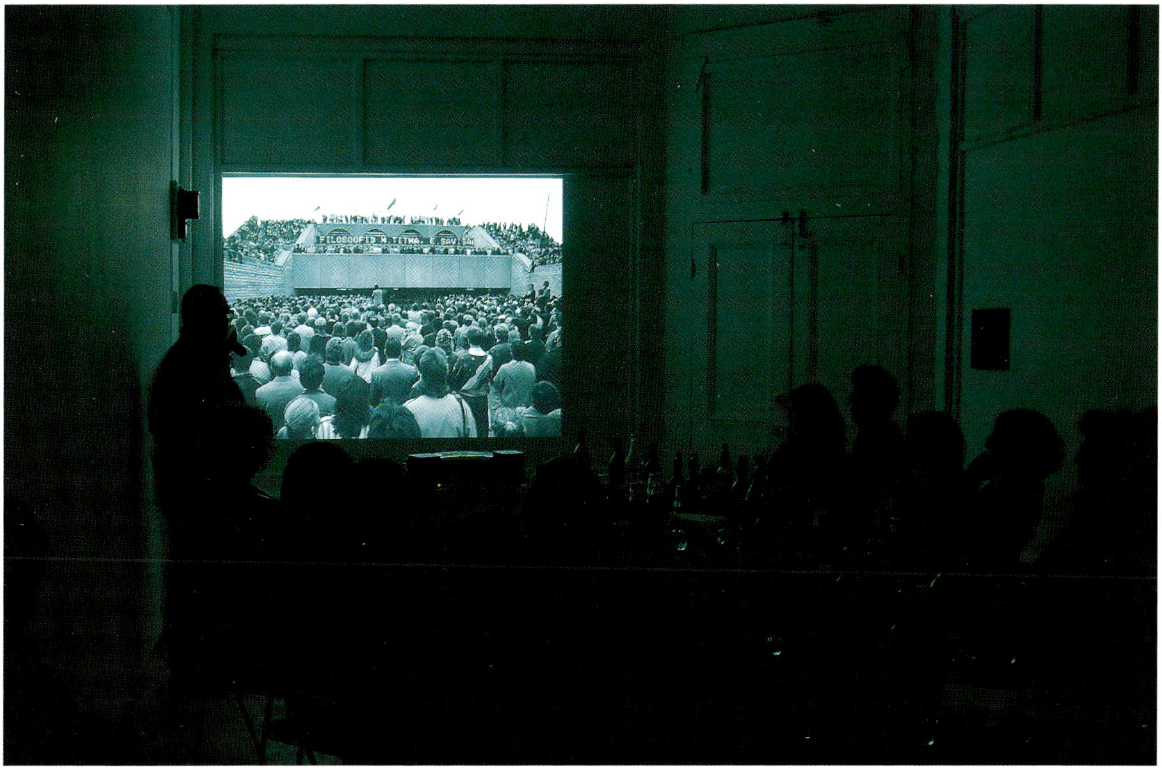

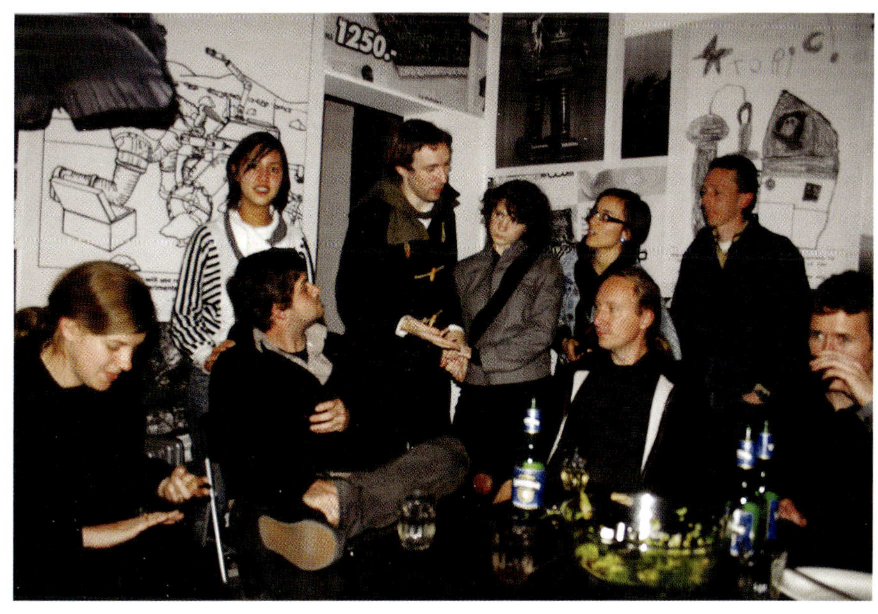
1250.-

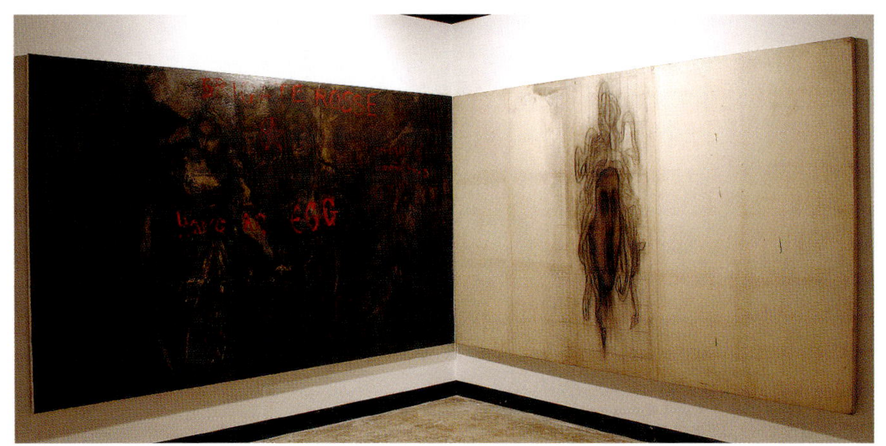

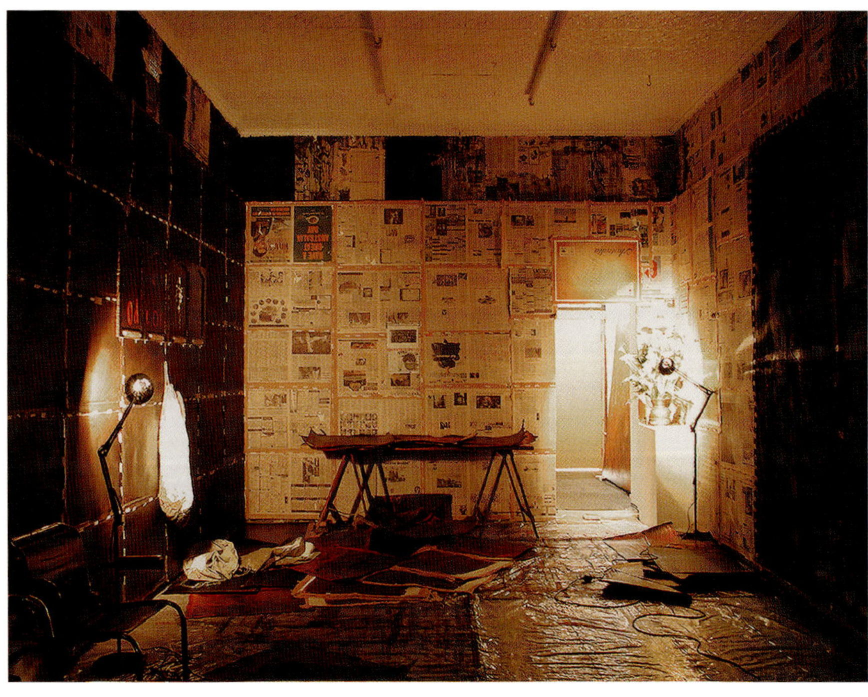

top:
Bernhard Sachs
Untitled
charcoal and acrylic on canvas
Ocular Lab: 12 at Spacement Gallery
2004

bottom:
Bernhard Sachs
Regime iconoclaste d'un frisson: le cercle vicieux après Salo
(*Iconoclastic Regime of the Shudder: the Vicious Circle after Salo*)
installation view
2005

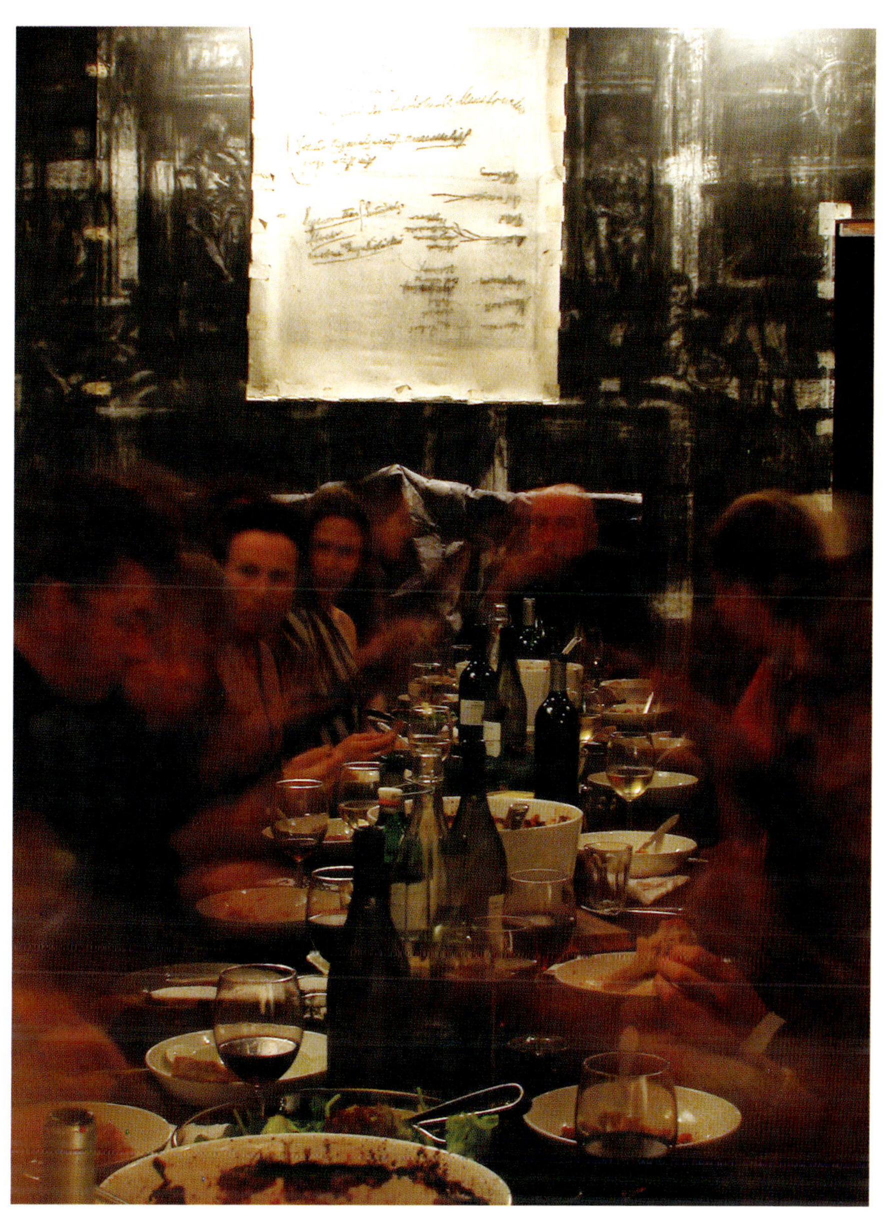

Bernhard Sachs
(Reconstruction of) The Polish Game
installation/action
detail of dinner (with Alex Rizkalla)
2004
photograph: Julie Davies

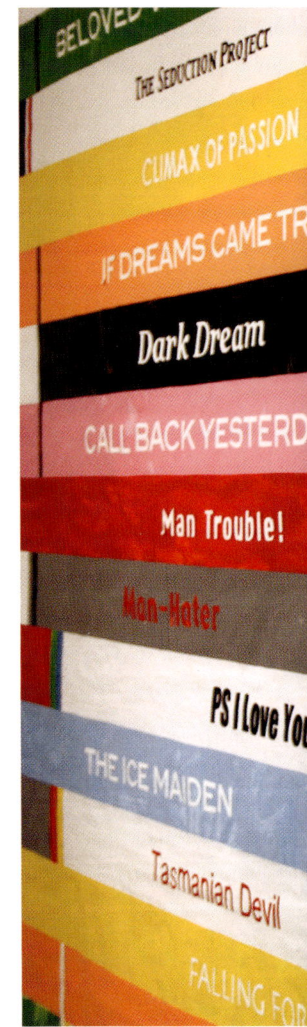

Louise Paramor
Letters, Lies, Alibis
acrylic paint on paper
Ocular Lab: 12 at Spacement Gallery
2005
courtesy the artist and Nellie Castan Gallery

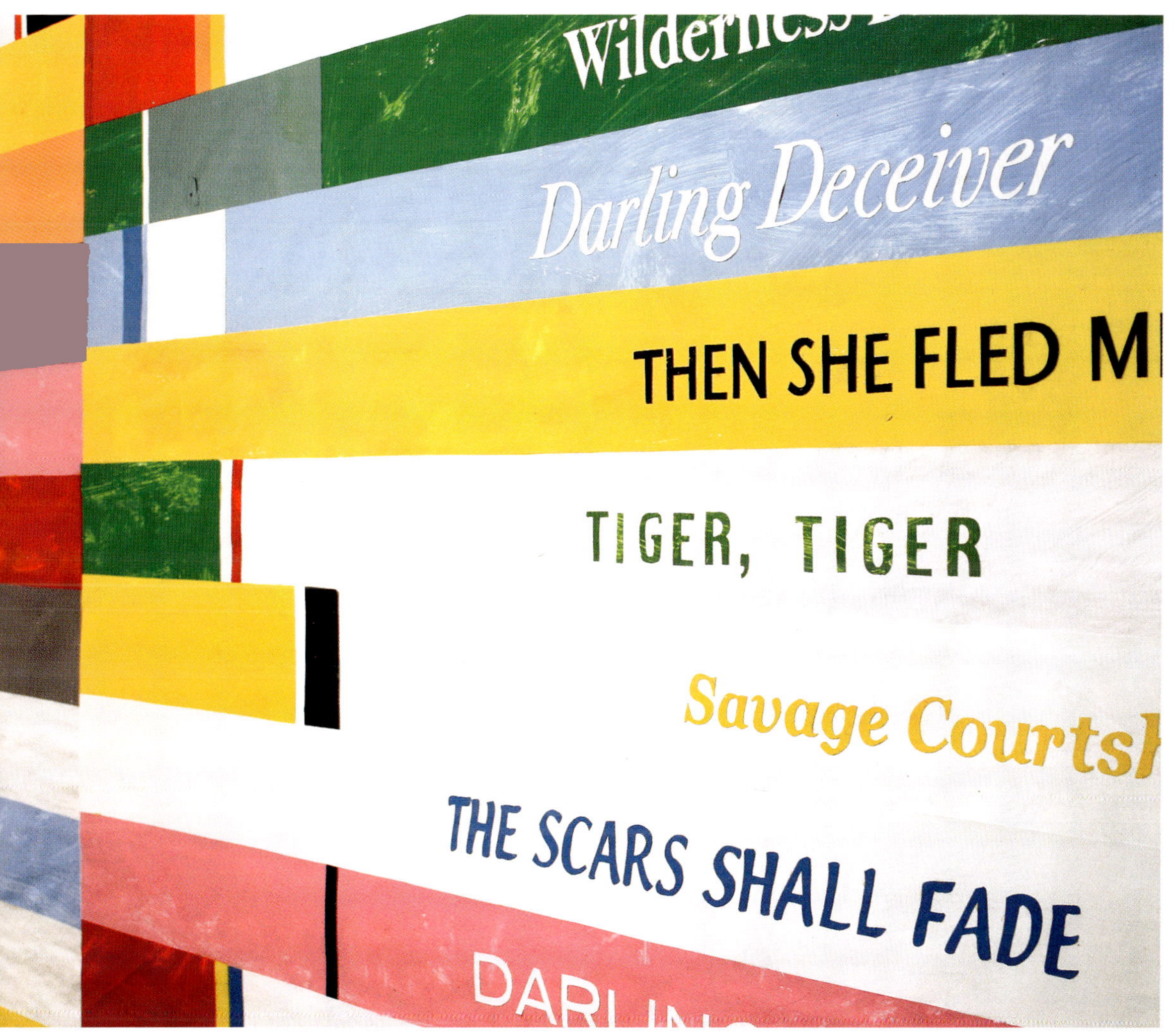
Darling Deceiver
THEN SHE FLED
TIGER, TIGER
Savage
THE SCARS SHALL FADE

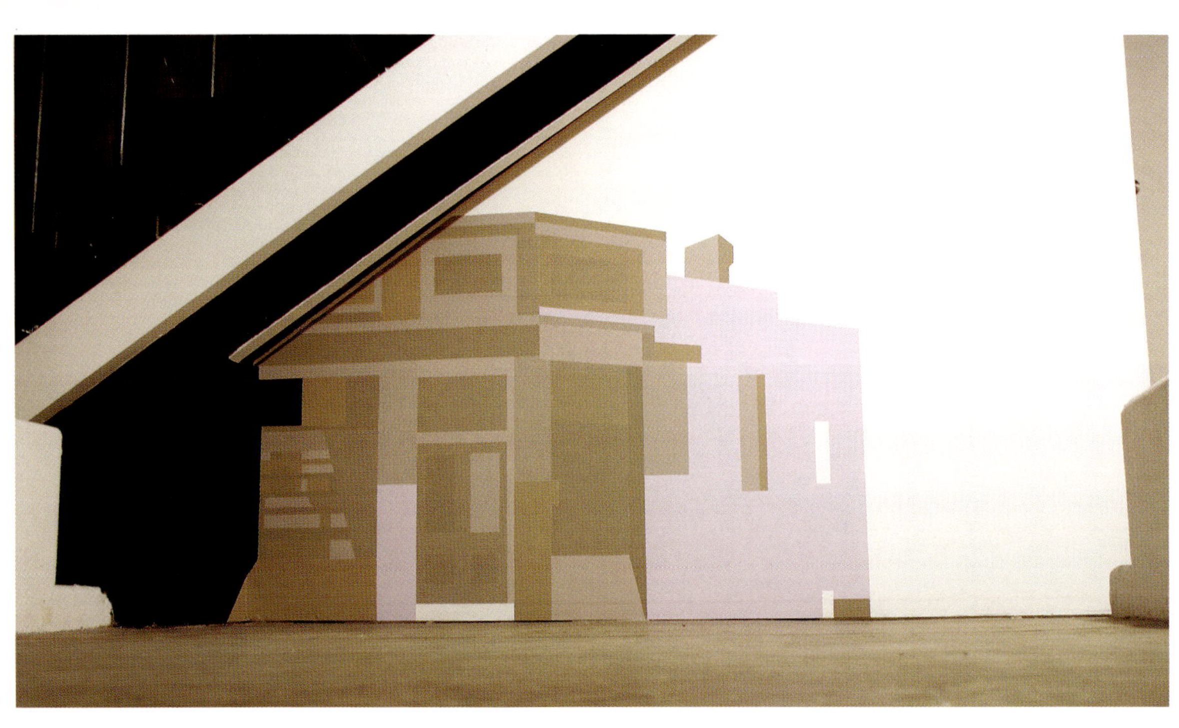

Raafat Ishak
Emergencies, Accidents and Congratulations
acrylic paint on wall
Ocular Lab: 12 at Spacement Gallery
2005

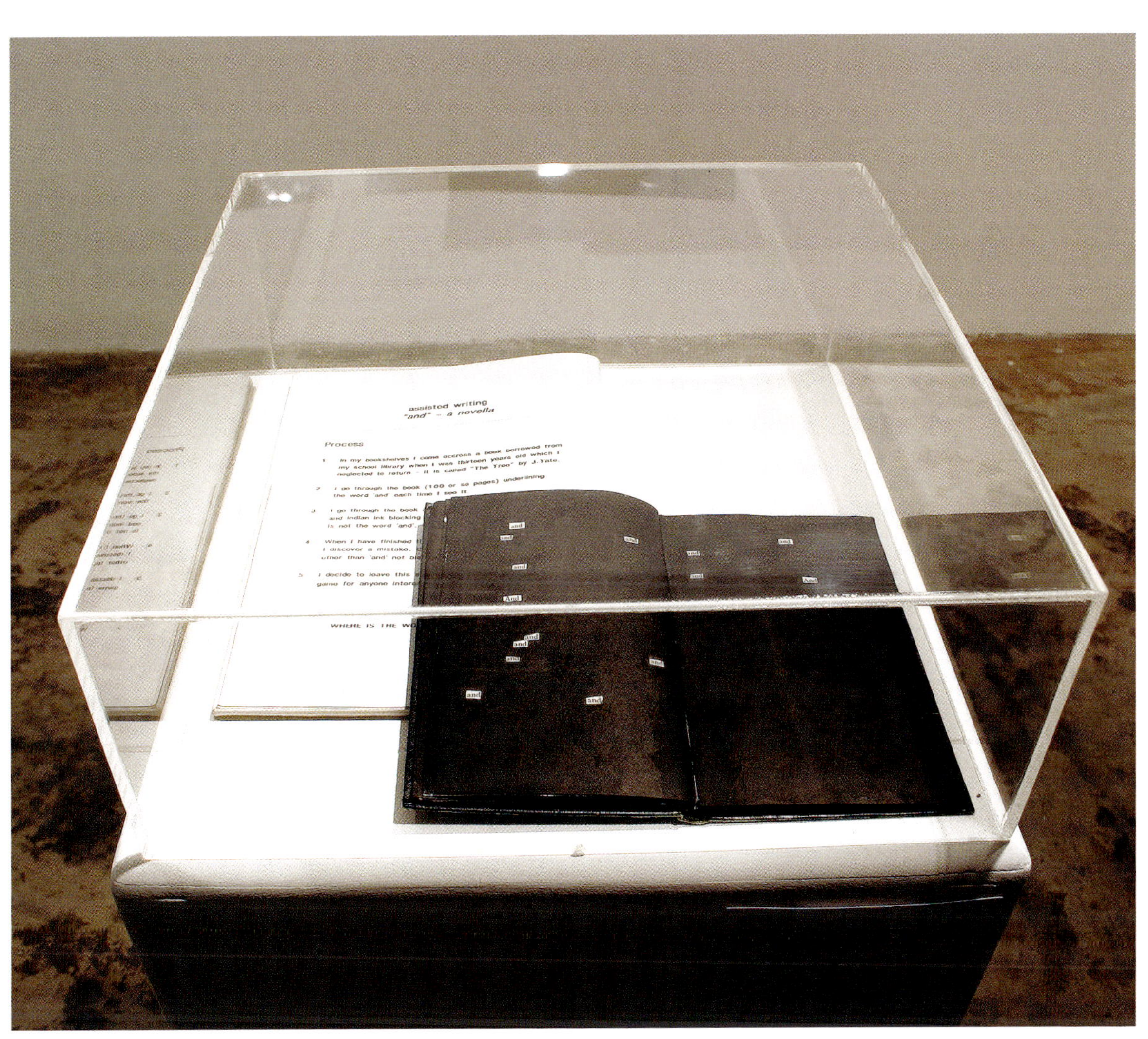

Sandra Bridie
Ian Matthews, 'and – a novella (a fiction)'
ink on paper
Ocular Lab: 12 at Spacement Gallery
1994

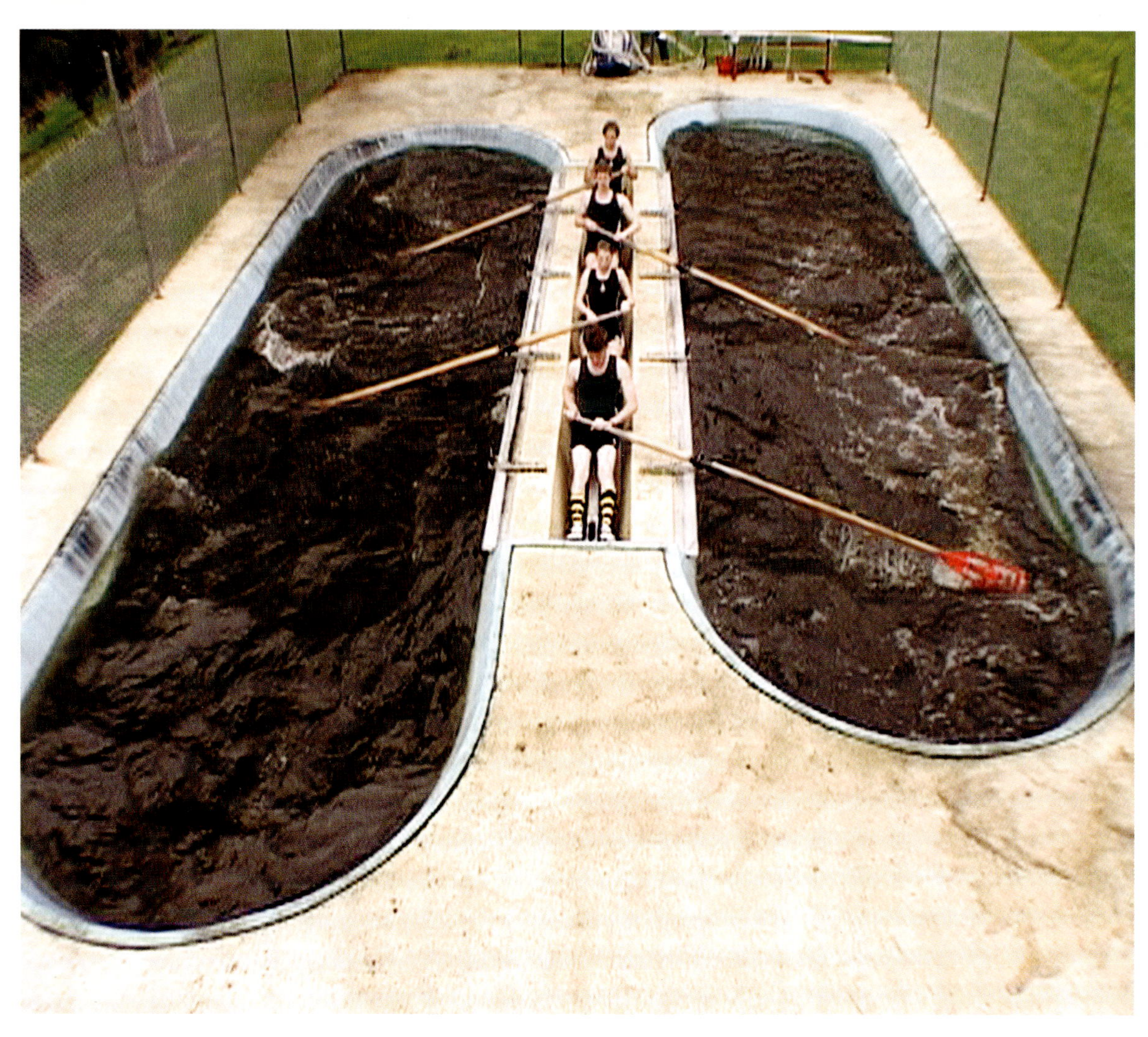

Sally Mannall
Untitled (The rowing project)
DVD
Trinity Nine at Trinity College, The University of Melbourne
2006

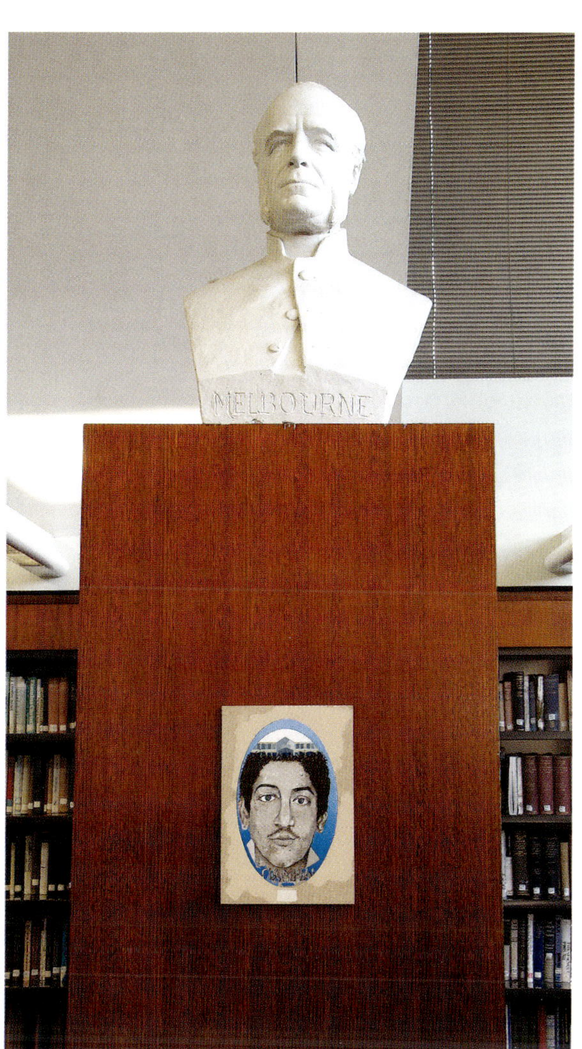

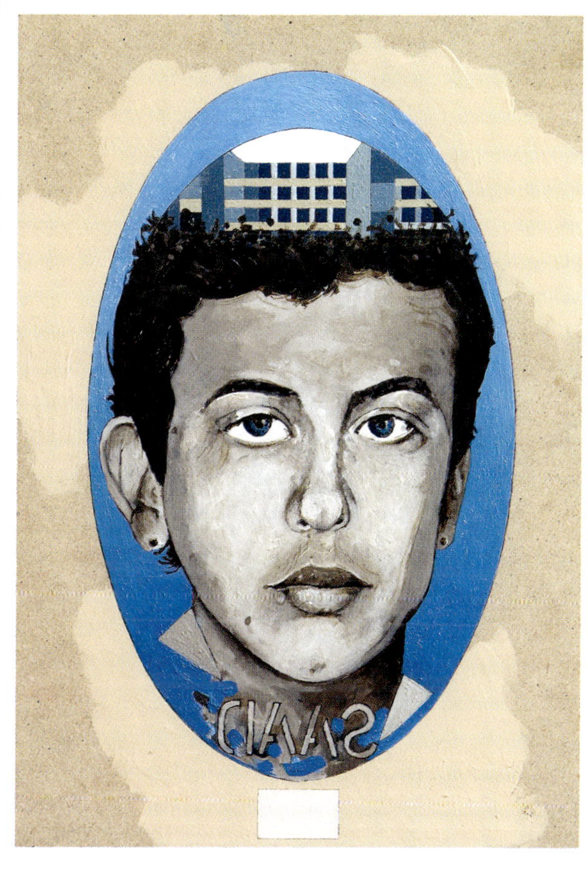

Raafat Ishak
Saad Cowan (1963)
acrylic and oil on MDF
Trinity Nine at Trinity College, The University of Melbourne
2006
photographs: Christian Capurro

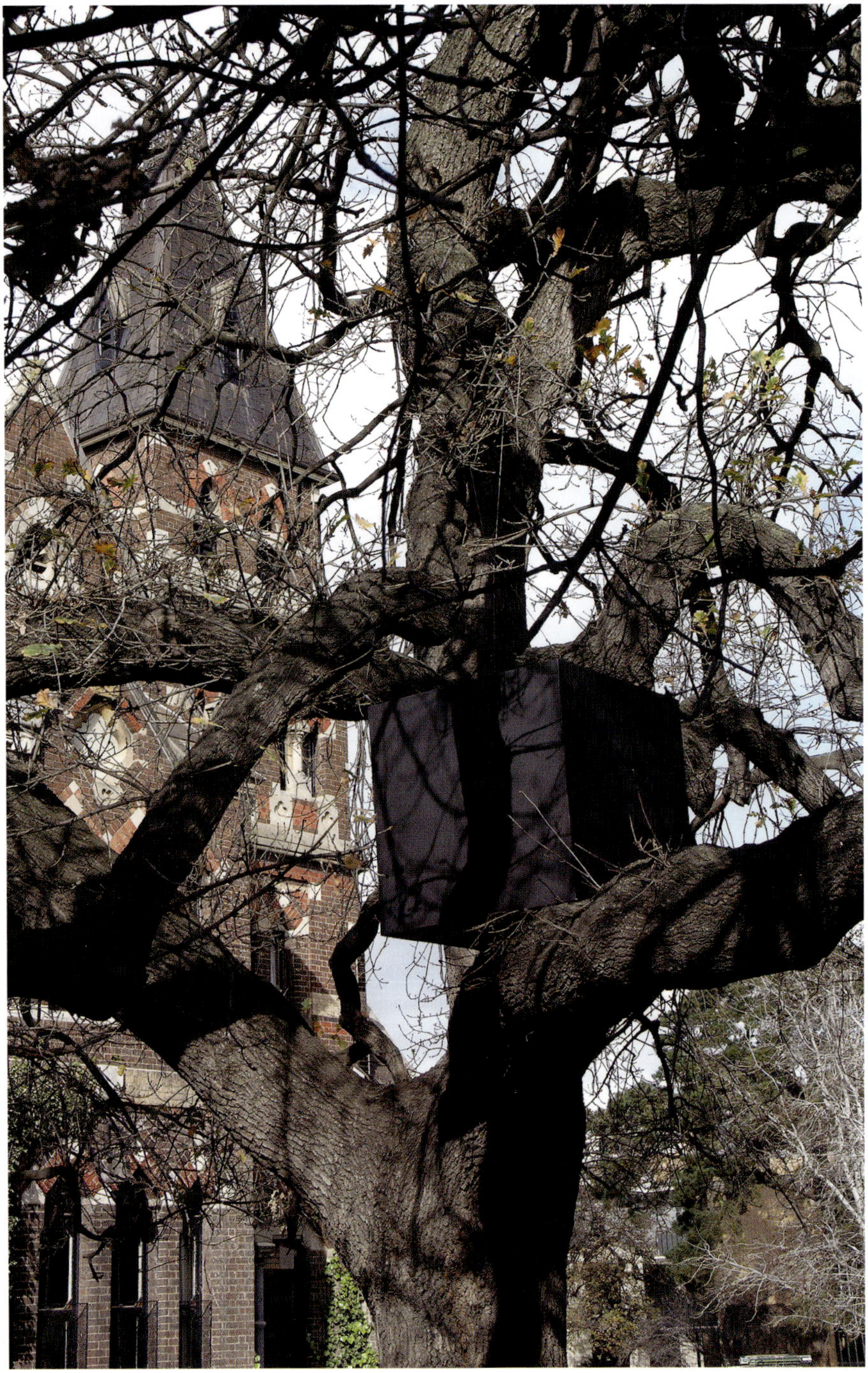

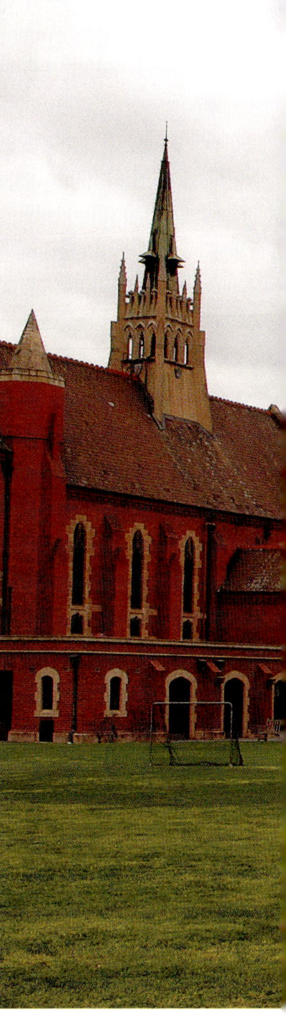

Raafat Ishak
Apparition of a mistake
acrylic on MDF (oak tree, college lawn)
Trinity Nine at Trinity College, The University of Melbourne
2006
photograph: Christian Capurro

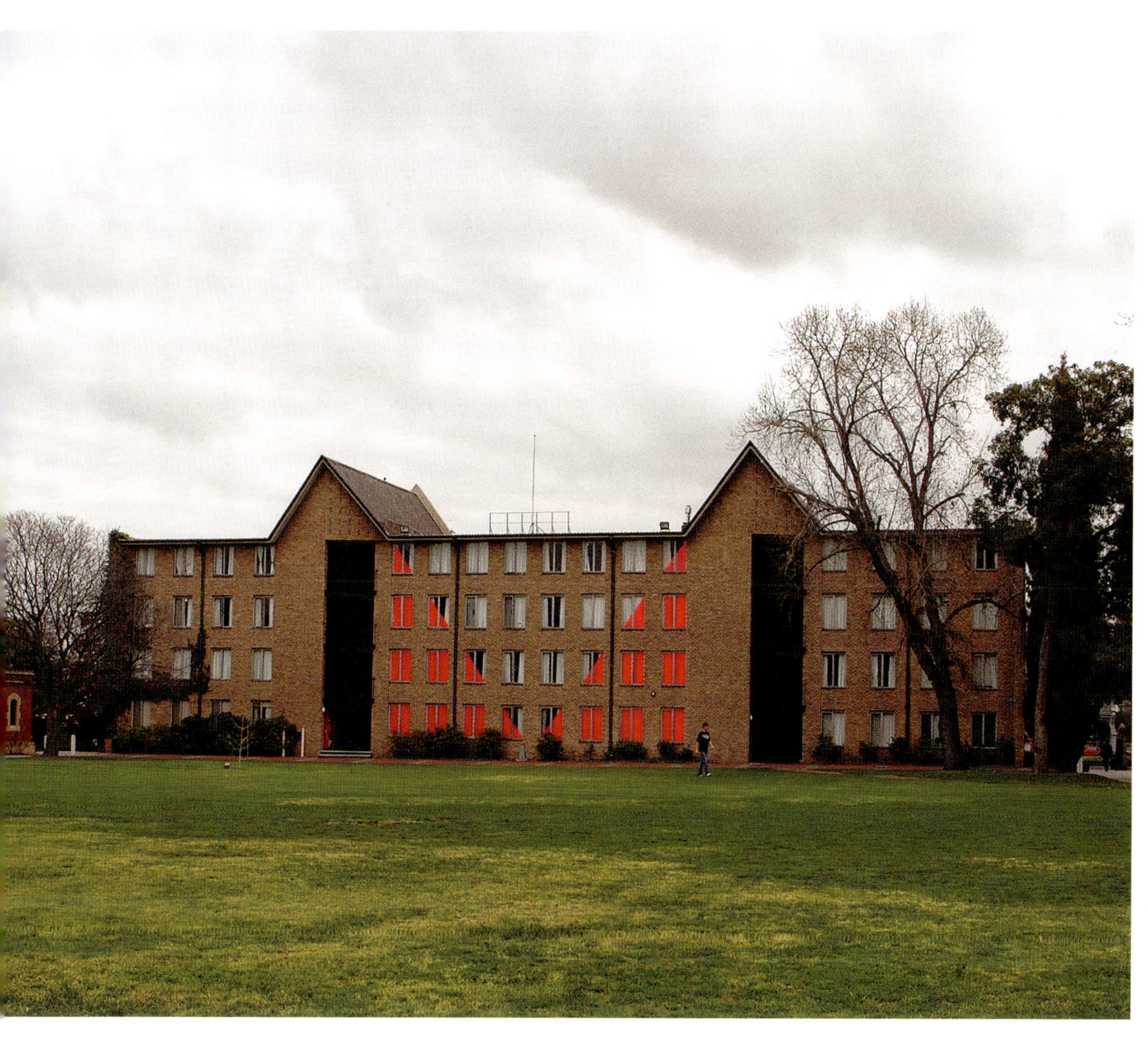

Sean Loughrey
Two Triangles, 20 Windows (Possible Things Project 2)
ripstop nylon, fluoro orange attachments
(Cowan Building facade)
Trinity Nine at Trinity College, The University of Melbourne
2006
photograph: Christian Capurro

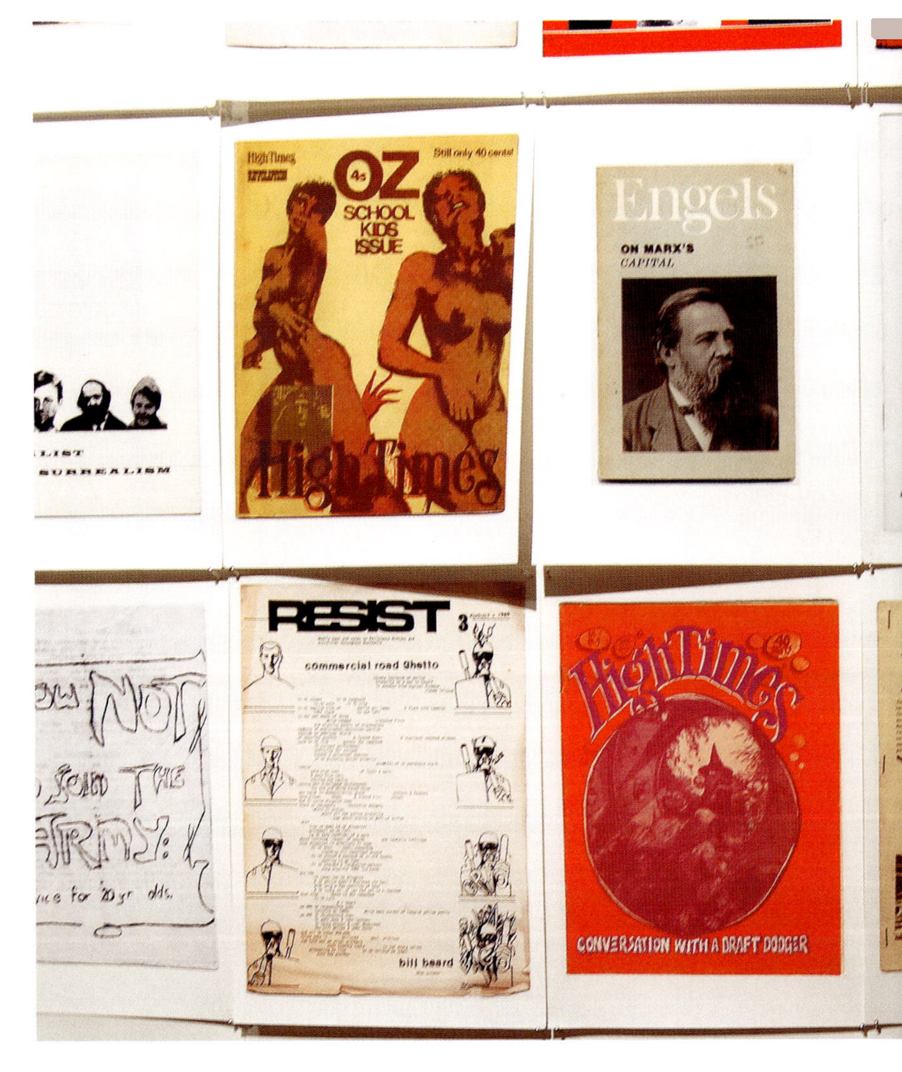

Alex Rizkalla
R is for Resistance
inkjet prints
Ocular Notes at George Paton Gallery
2007
courtesy the artist and Place Gallery

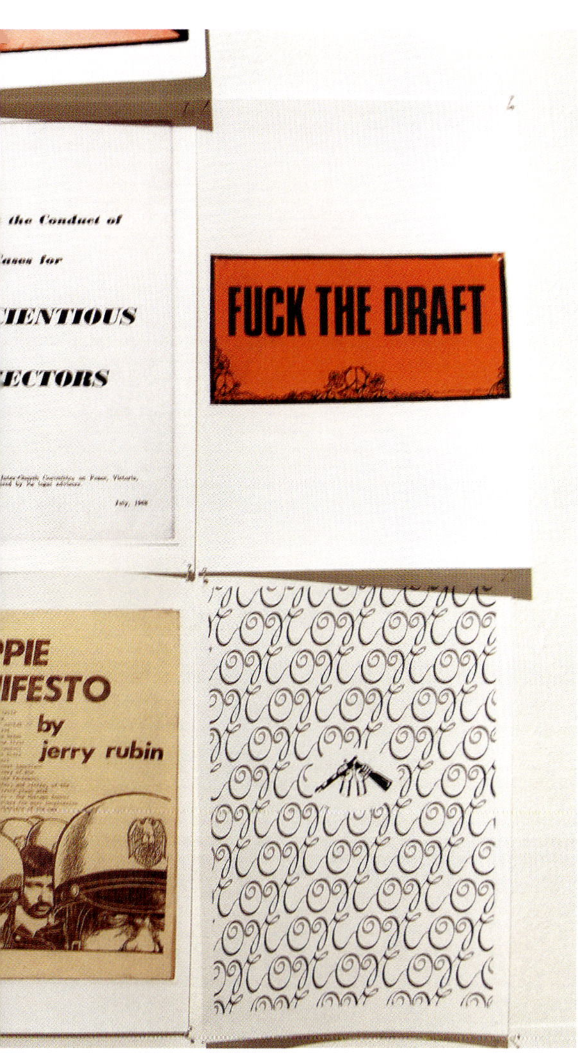

the Conduct of
ases for
IENTIOUS
ECTORS
FUCK THE DRAFT
PIE
IFESTO
by
jerry rubin

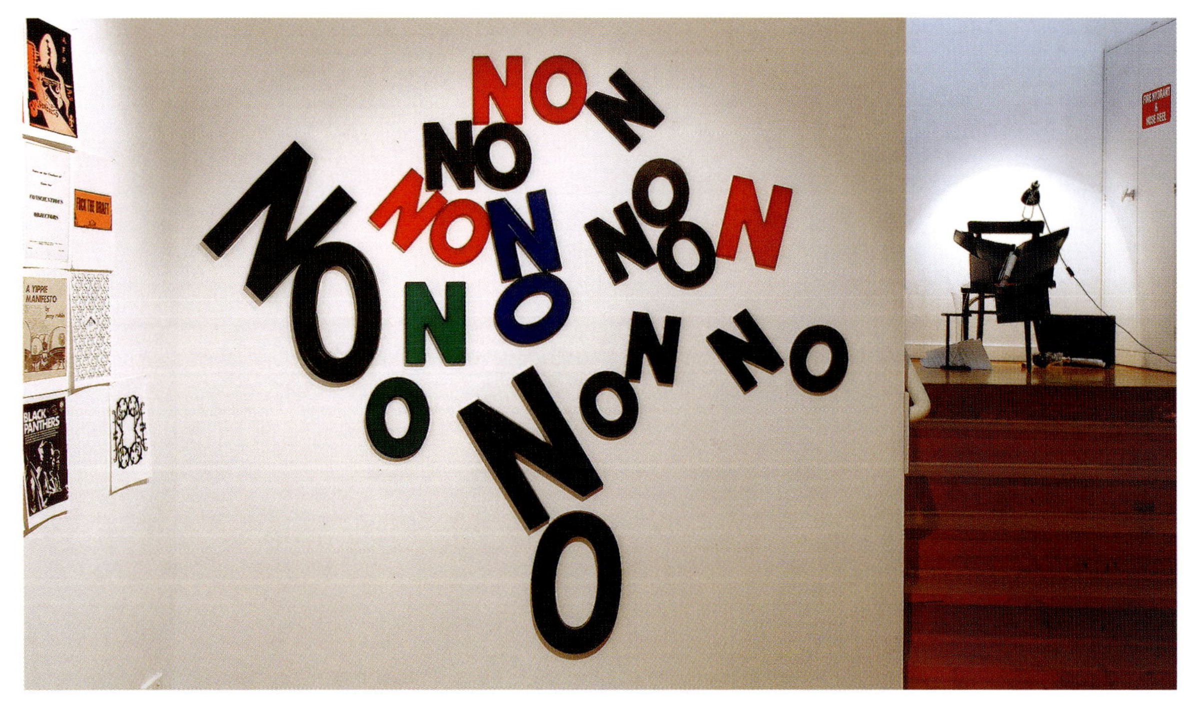

Alex Rizkalla
R is for Resistance
plastic letters
Ocular Notes at George Paton Gallery
2007
courtesy the artist and Place Gallery

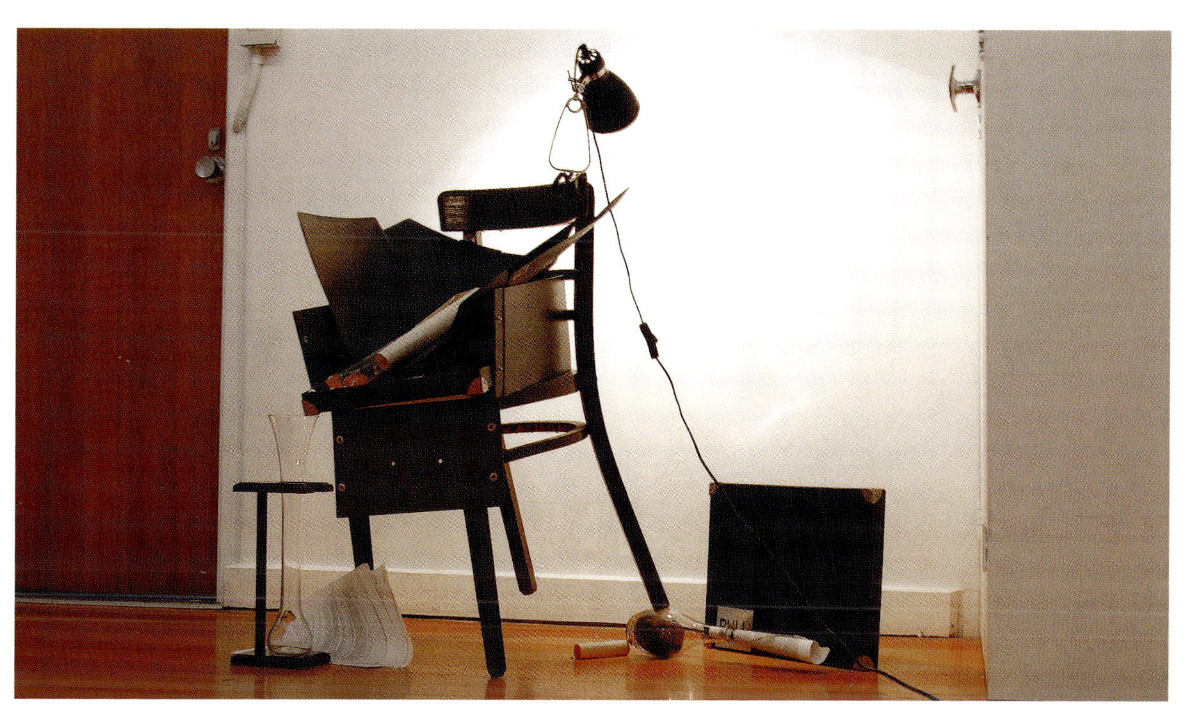

John Abbate
Untitled
assembled piece with chair, file box, file folders, paper, lamp, glass vases,
photocopy toner and bed sheet
Ocular Notes at George Paton Gallery
2007

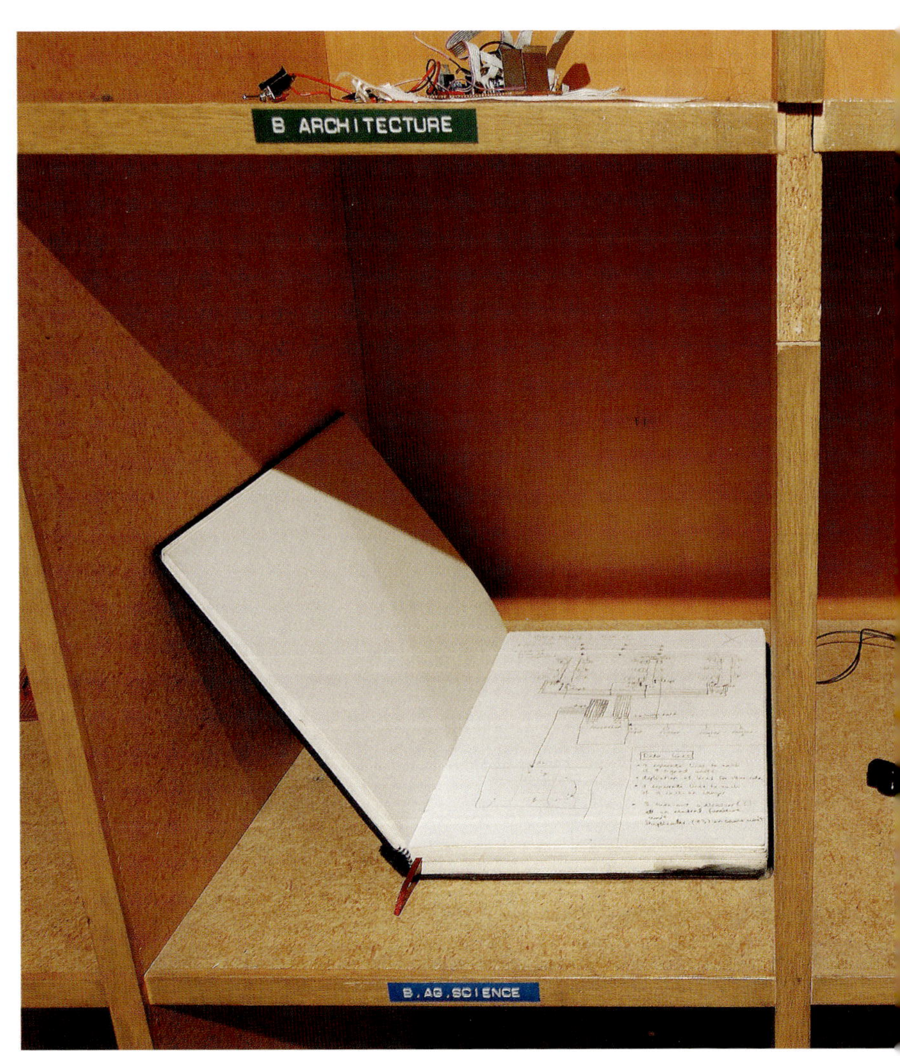

Jonathan Luker
40 failed/discontinued experiments (detail)
Ocular Notes at George Paton Gallery
2007

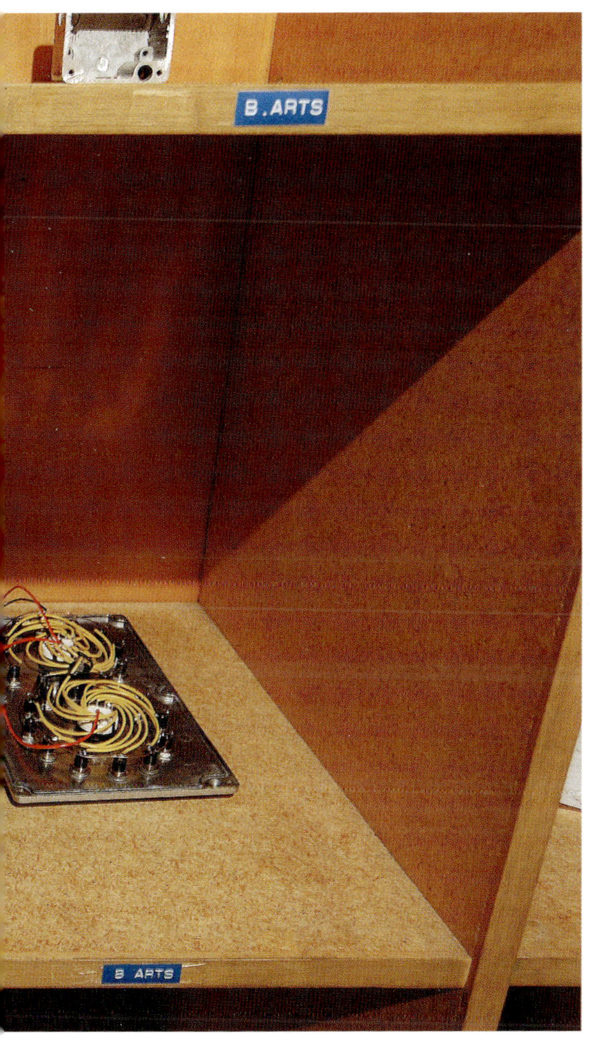
B.ARTS
B ARTS

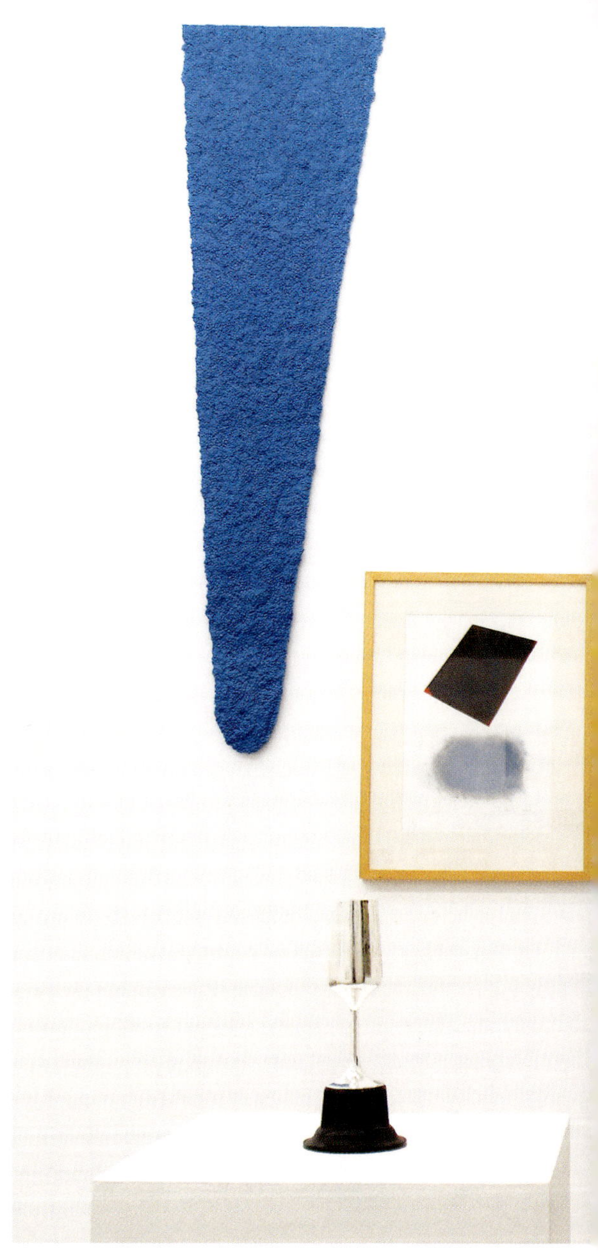

Ocular Lab Inc. fundraiser, 2008

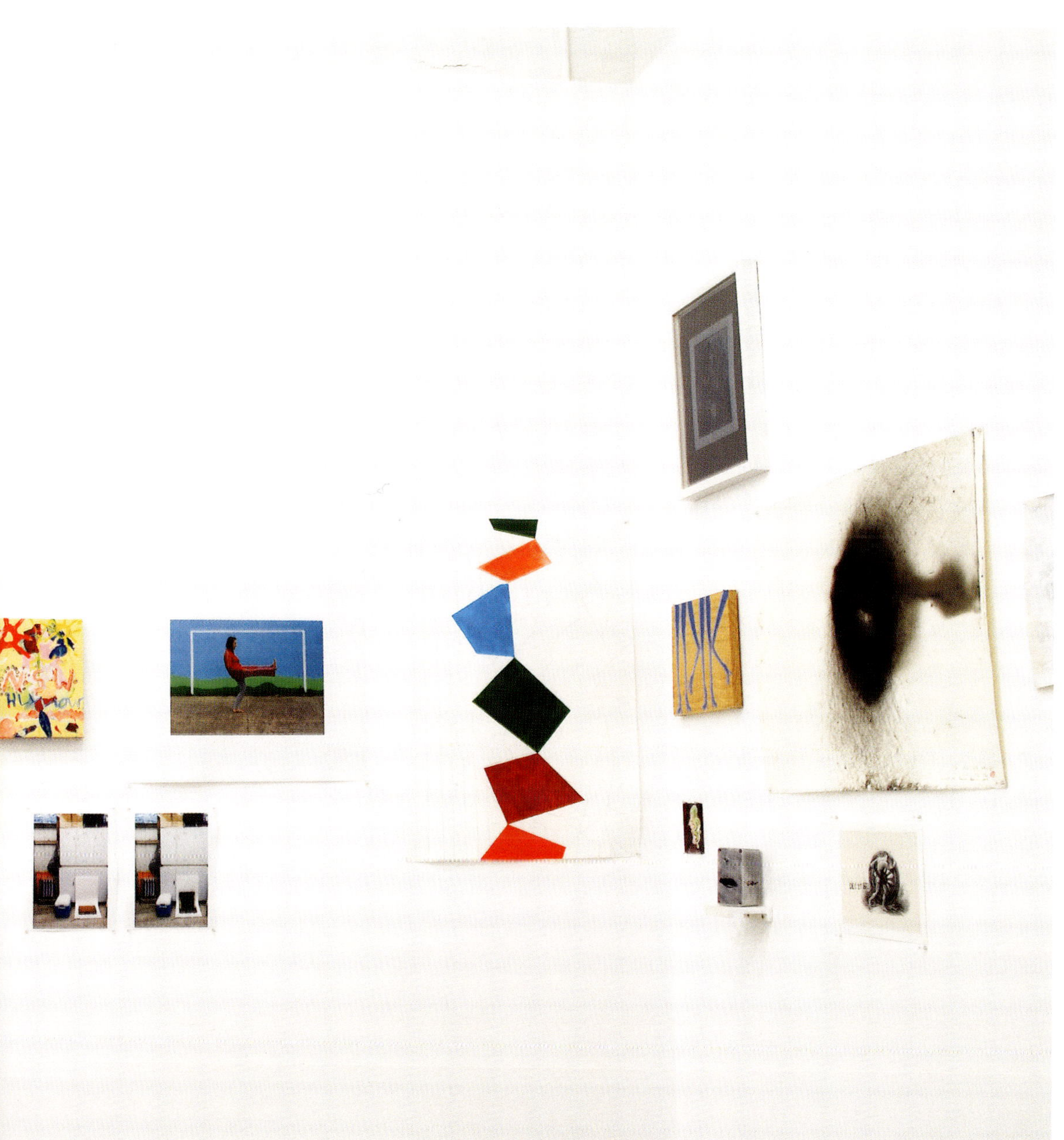

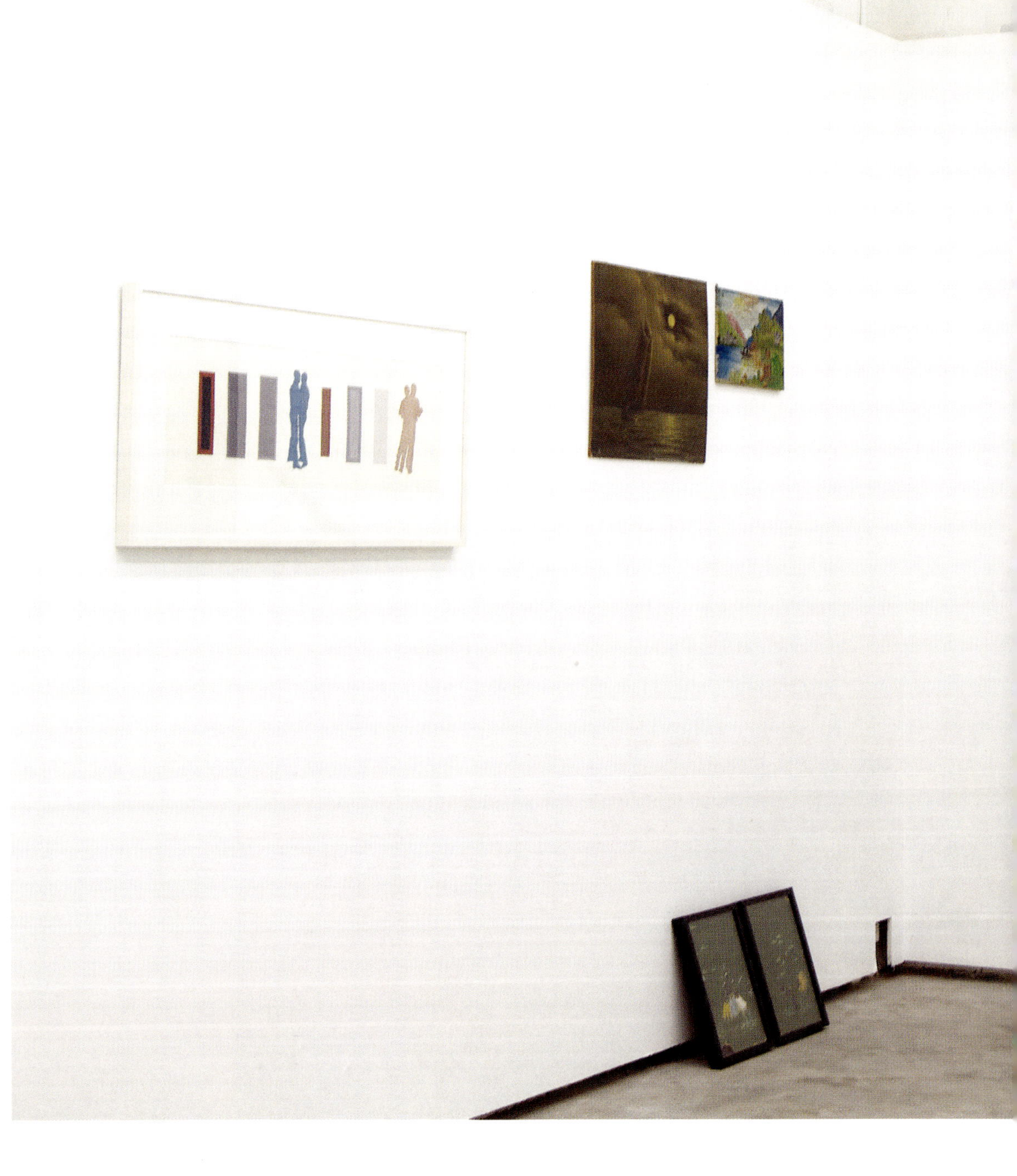

The Collection Show
artworks from the collections of: Sally Mannall, Raafat Ishak
and Elvis Richardson
2009

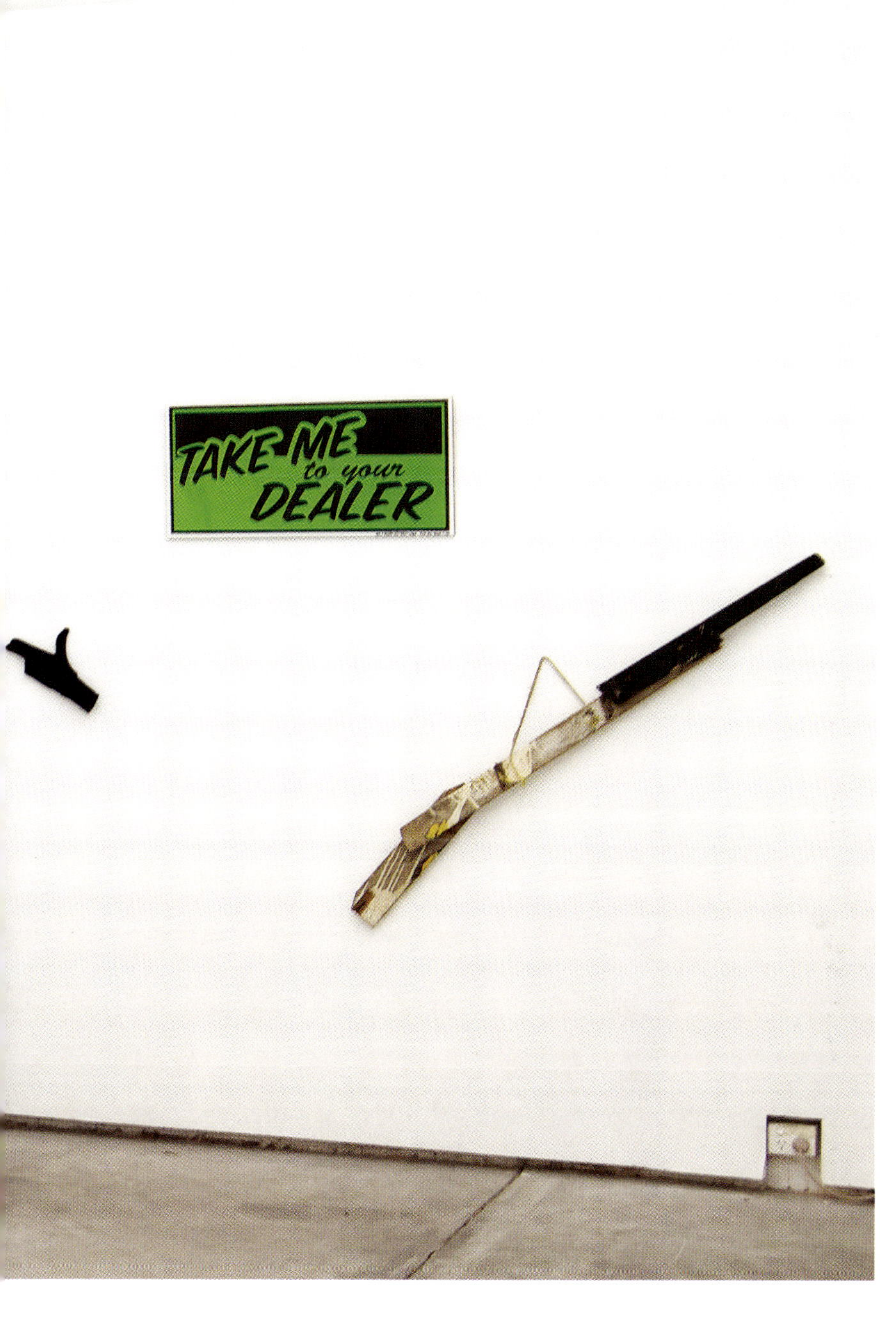
TAKE ME
to your
DEALER

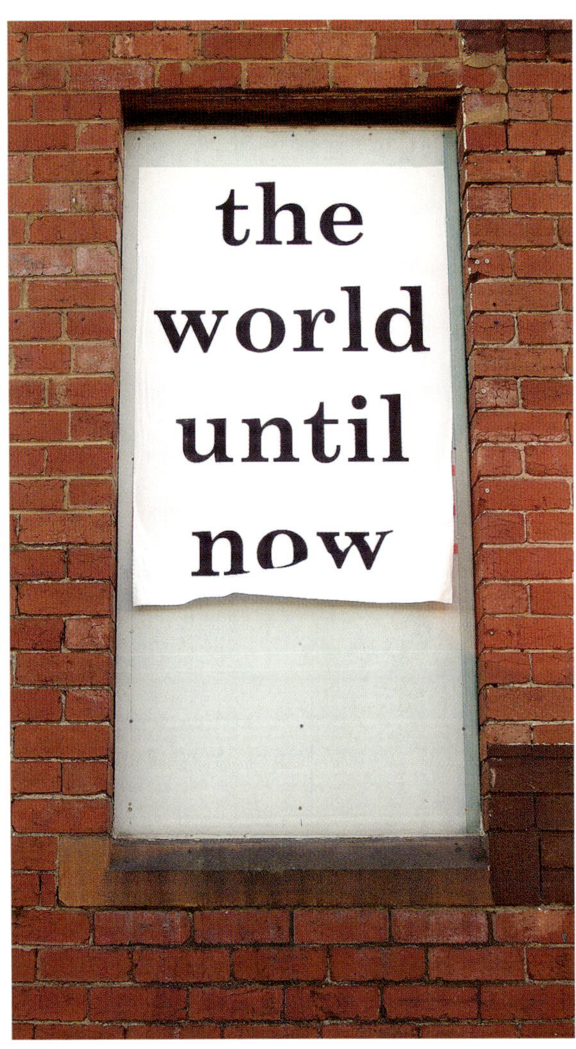

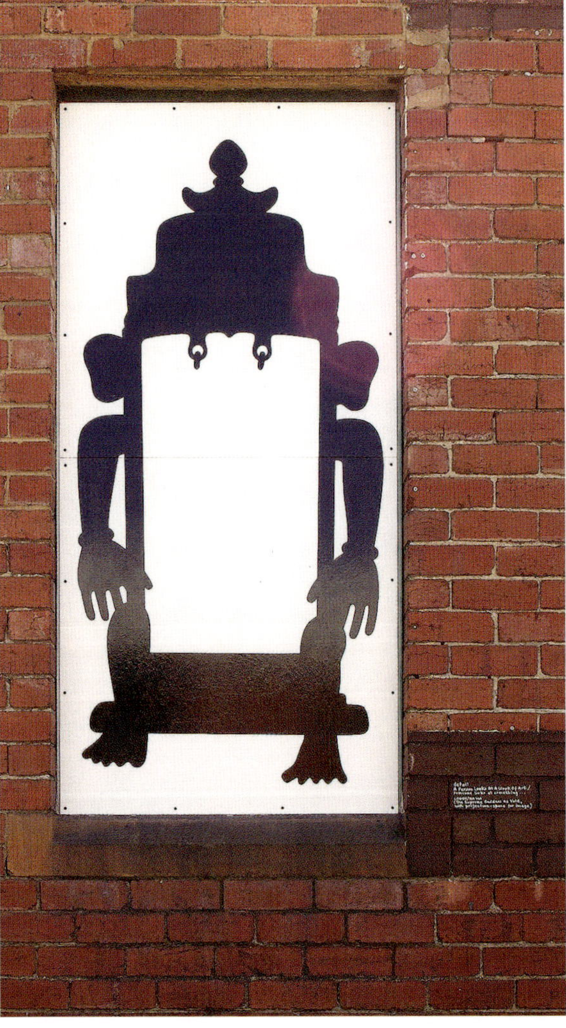

Billboards
above left: Andrew McQualter
above right and right: Peter Tyndall
opposite: Cameron Robbins

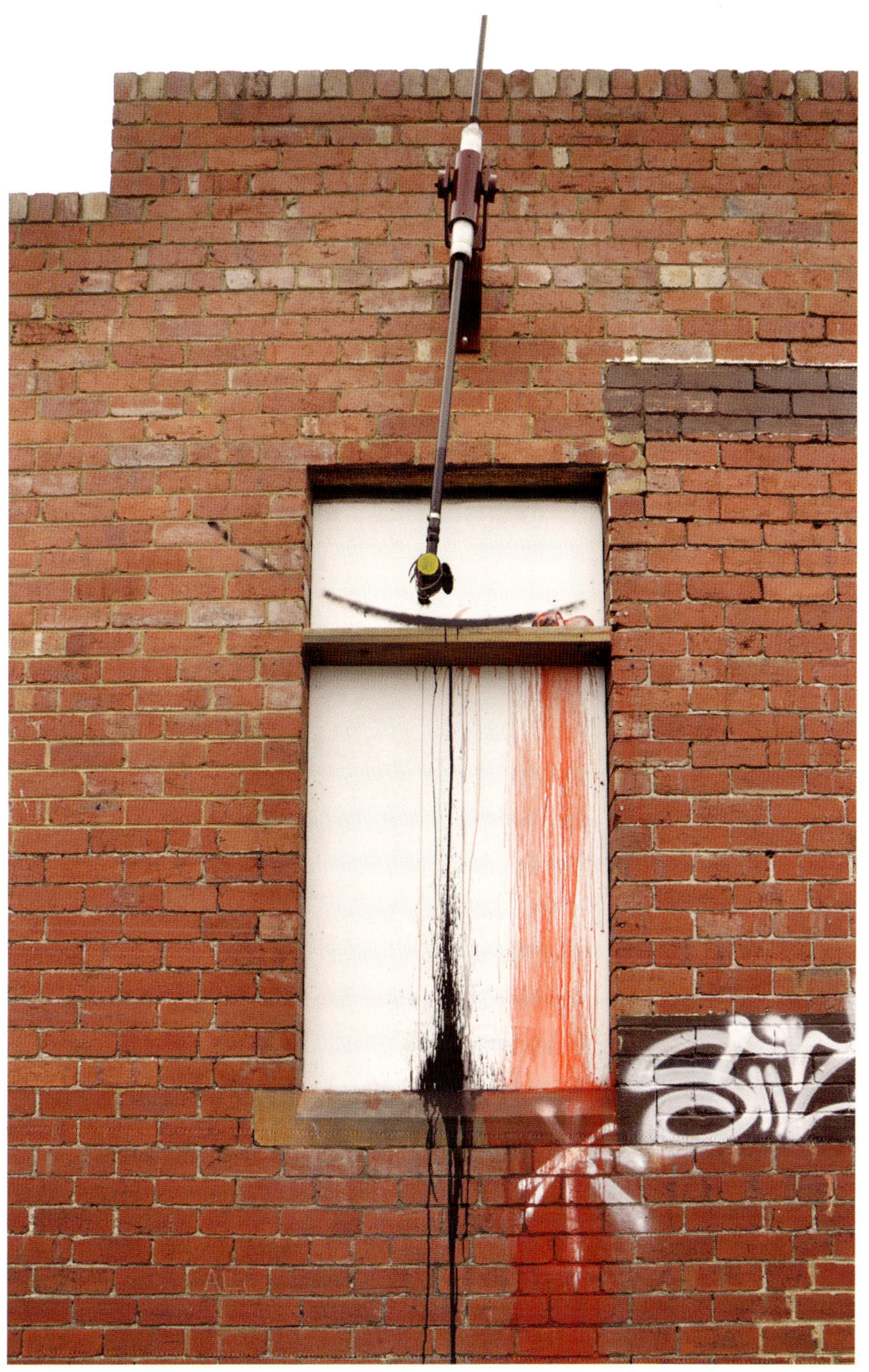

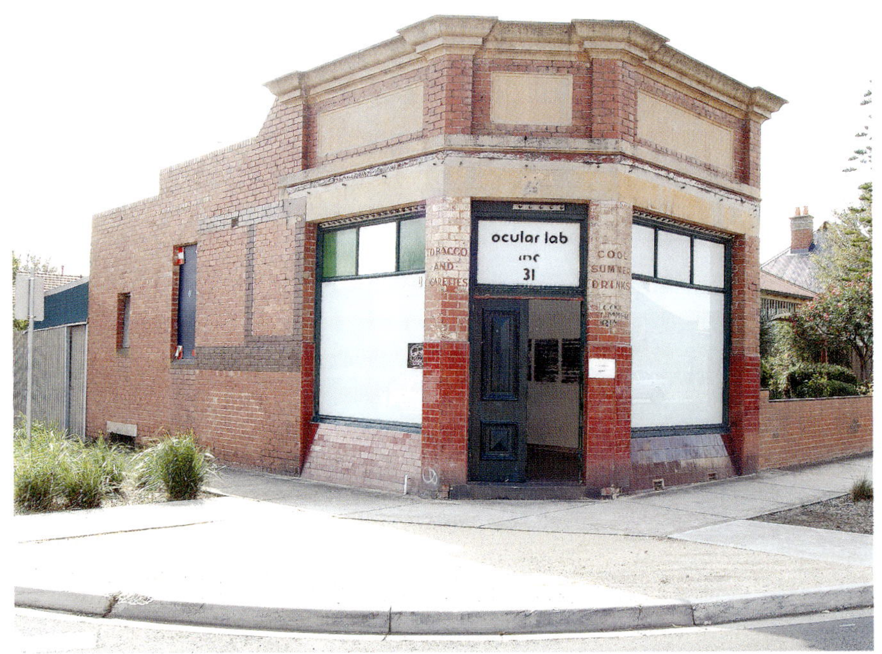

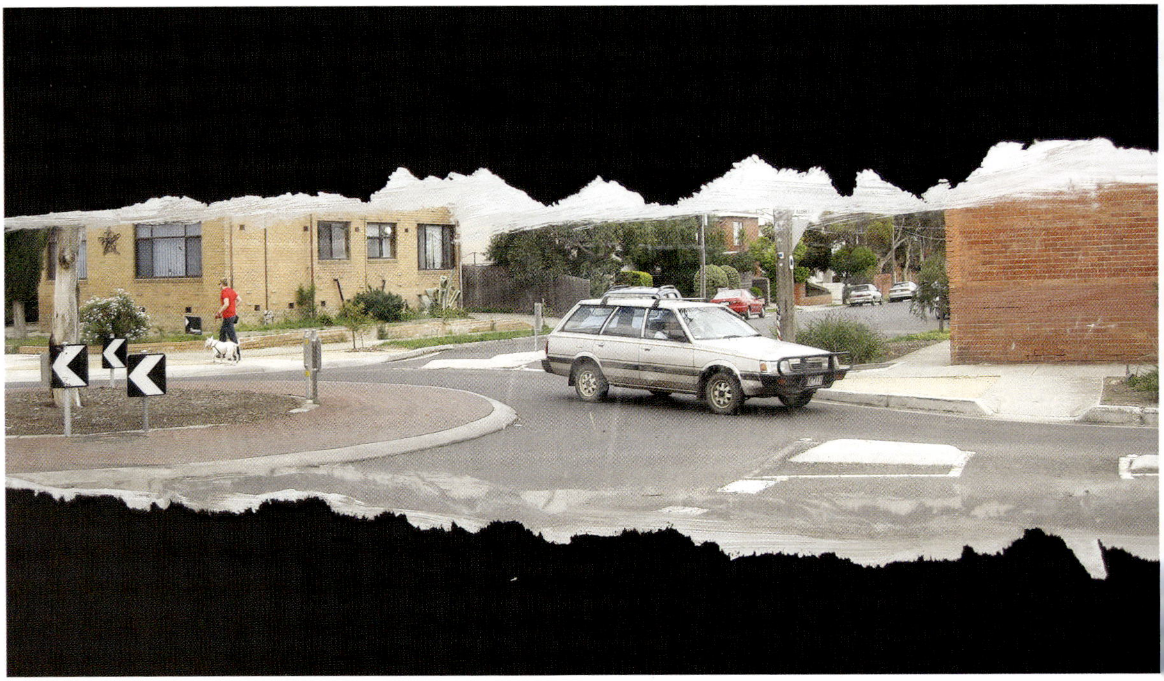

top:
Ocular Lab Inc.
photograph: Jan Svenungsson

bottom:
Lisa Kelly
The Lab
2009

TEXTS

WHERE IS CONTEMPORARY ART?

Stephen Zagala

Ocular Lab was an inclusive artistic collective that created a physical presence for itself around an old corner milk bar in the residential backstreets of Brunswick. Converted into a site for contemporary art projects, the disused store was fondly referred to as 'the Lab' and spoken about as a facility that provided conditions for artistic research, experimentation and dialogue.

Sometimes the Lab looked like an art gallery, but it was really a multi-purpose venue that functioned as a communal restaurant, a meeting room, a studio and a library. Different exhibitions transformed the gallery space into something more like a cinema, a live theatre or a garage sale. The internal gravitas of the collective made the space feel like the headquarters of a clandestine arts guild, but it also maintained an open relationship with the street; you could enter through the double doors on the corner or through a courtyard at the rear, a billboard space brought art projects to the pavement, and the shop windows were treated as an aperture that could be painted over or stripped clean. It occupied the neighbourhood like a quietly evolving crystalline form, refracting and reflecting its milieu through a multi-faceted prism of activity.

Writing as someone who participated in this milieu, it is easier to celebrate Ocular Lab's *modus operandi* than to provide an overview of its achievements. This conundrum pivots on the Lab's commitment to fostering creative processes above and beyond any specific product.

Artist-run initiatives (ARIs) often give voice to experimental ideals, and talk the talk of liberation from art-world institutions, but most are satisfied to add a DIY patina to organisational structures and objectives that have been derived from commercial or public galleries. Ocular Lab seemed to go further than most ARIs in its commitment to artistic experimentation, independent discourse and community-based networks. In the absence of a guiding manifesto or even an organisational structure, the Lab operated in a purposefully intuitive way, supporting lateral lines of creative enquiry through an open-ended, face-to-face network of creatives. The achievements and outcomes were consequently embedded in localised processes, which undoubtably continue to inform the creative trajectories and collaborative relationships of the Lab's participants. This is worth celebrating in itself, even if the contour of tangible outcomes remains imperceptible.

If we step back from the Lab's own milieu, however, this perspective seems overly naïve and lacking in critical context. ARIs have proliferated over the last three decades and now clearly constitute an institutional stratum of the Contemporary Art movement. There are over 100 active ARIs in Australia today, with about a third of these located in Melbourne. The Australia Council for the Arts and Arts Victoria have developed funding structures to support this echelon of activity, and professional advocates of Contemporary Art have come to rely on the resources that ARIs provide.

Art historians interested in the lineage of independent art collectives in Melbourne can trace their genesis back to the founding of the Contemporary Art Society in 1938. In the 1950s and 1960s, a succession of art collectives were forged in opposition to the 'establishment', and maker-galleries began to emerge in the late 1960s and 1970s. When John Nixon set up Art Projects in 1979, bringing a shrewdly professional approach to the idea of an 'alternative' gallery space, the stage was set for the subsequent canonisation of an artist-run scene in Melbourne. It is prudent to recognise that Ocular Lab was established by artists who had been actively engaging in this scene for some time, and their resistance to organisational structures and user-pay economics can be viewed as an implicit critique of how ARIs have been professionalised since the 1980s.

It seems pertinent to note that the historical rise of ARIs is coextensive with the evolution of global economic systems, which (among other things) willingly trade in intangible commodities. We now live in a world where ephemeral experiences can be commodified and quite effectively incorporated into the market (think iTunes, think eco-tourism, think art biennales, think video art). Ironically (if not comically), ARIs have often asserted their experimental status in opposition to a world that was disappearing just as they arrived, a world where an artist's economic viability had to be stretched on canvas or cast in bronze.

In contrast to this type of positioning, Ocular Lab's credentials were established at a methodological level — in the way they did things — rather than in the forms of art that were exhibited. By taking this approach, the Lab not only avoided jousting with windmills, it was able to pursue a genuinely experimental line of flight. Instead of making essentialist statements in the form of 'this is who we are', Ocular Lab asked the creative questions: 'how, when and where might contemporary art exist?'

31 PEARSON STREET, WEST BRUNSWICK 3055 [MAP REF 29 7D]

Zara Stanhope

> Involvement in an ARI is a rite of passage.[1]
> — Raafat Ishak

Microcosms within microcosms, artist collectives or initiatives are organisms injected into the veins of visual art. Despite artists' intentions of independence, short- and long-term collaborations can cohere into a nutrient that sustains the corpus of art — an unacknowledged and undervalued support system. Generally, artist-run initiatives (ARIs) pump with youthful blood, their members gathering together for support, agency or a common purpose. Energy is an indispensable ARI feature: constituents and audiences alike require stamina to sustain the organisation and the vigour to experience what develops. Most are relatively short-lived, prey to the results of the maturation process they facilitate. The characteristic temporality of ARIs — here today, gone tomorrow — contributes to the limited understanding of their operation and effect. From a cultural perspective, artists' collaborations appear as generic units — each is differentiated by its members or purpose, but, on the whole, they appear as equivalent cells enriching a larger organ. However, regardless of duration (and Melbourne has fine examples of longevity in Platform and West Space), ARIs are typically self-determining and oppositional, established against the existing industry system of museums, private and commercial galleries and even other ARIs.[2]

The administrative tasks of communication and documentation can rank low in the face of the necessity of keeping an ARI running, exacerbating the risk of the oversight of these tasks. To gain a comprehensive understanding of Ocular Lab Inc. would have required infiltrating this ARI's anatomy: being at the group meetings, viewing ninety-three exhibitions, attending the events and subsequent social gatherings. This text was an opportunity to record one trace of the six-year life of 'the Lab', through the reflections of its organising members, in the hope of offering an internal reference, a Lab-biosis, a narrative that will assist in differentiating Ocular Lab.

OCULAR LABORATORY

> The fact that an old milk bar can be a space for experimental art was enough for me.
> — Sean Loughrey

ARIs are fertile hubs, contexts that germinate new developments in art practice and encourage experimentation; they are, by nature, testing grounds. Ocular Lab Inc. had its genesis in the evolving interests and activities of artists Julie Davies and Alex Rizkalla, most conspicuously in their desire to explore ways to increase collegiality. Ocular Lab Inc. (the Lab) was the offspring of the earlier Ocular Laboratory, a year-long project that began in September 1997, which arose from a preceding initiative of Davies and Rizkalla: *h. Project*. Operating in a commercial building in the Melbourne suburb of St Kilda, *h. Project* presented exhibitions and projects by Australian and overseas artists, in its *raison d'être* to activate some of the networks and ideas that the two artists had developed, including European connections that had germinated from contact with Fritz Rahmann and the collective Burö Berlin, as well as invigorating artists' networks.[3] It succeeded in this and in exposing Melbourne audiences to art from elsewhere but, according to Davies and Rizkalla, it sacrificed flexibility in overdetermining exhibition programming.

Their subsequent project space, Ocular Laboratory, which opened in 1999, was located in what had been the couple's studio space in a former milk bar on Pearson Street, West Brunswick. Over twelve months, Ocular Laboratory hosted works by artists including Raafat Ishak, Bernhard Sachs, Sally Mannall and Sean Loughrey — mutual friends and colleagues who would continue their involvement. Ultimately, Ocular Laboratory did not fulfil the search for more intensive discursive interaction. What was missing, and what would distinguish its successor, Ocular Lab Inc., was the shared intersubjectivity that Davies, Rizkalla and other colleagues sought to enlarge the concept of art practice. Plans grew over the subsequent three years for a reorganised collaboration that could inform, test and establish relations across practice and theory.

CONVENING A COMMUNITY

ARIs, by nature, originate amongst friends or like-minded associates sharing a common purpose.[4] These constituents — artists who had previously collaborated with Davies and Rizkalla or other members — were the genesis of the Lab and its point of difference. By early 2003, a group was coordinated through common interests and Melbourne art networks: Sean Loughrey shared contacts with Burö Berlin and German artists; Sandra Bridie was interested in international artist-run models and had been a key member of *Talk Artists Initiative* in the 1990s; Loughrey, Ishak, Mannall and Sachs had been Ocular Laboratory participants, and they encouraged others such as Tom Nicholson to become involved. Individuals had their own reasons for joining, but all shared with Davies and Rizkalla a political leaning that can be generalised as situated in a left-of-centre oppositional sensibility and a critique of neoliberalism. Sachs shared an appreciation of a context that included 'a number of members of non-Anglo-Saxon backgrounds, reflective of a "New Australia" ... and shared interests in migration, and concern with the representation and translations of history'.[5]

The function of the Lab — a space for open-ended experimentation, and operating a little like a left-wing think tank — was of interest to curator and arts writer Kirsten Rann. She conceived an alignment with the Lab's philosophy and the members' focus 'on discourse/discussion. Many of their projects were socio-politically active (critical) and that provided an alternative model to sanctioned institutional and practising structures.' Rann's inclusion in the initial membership was in contrast to the organisation's general disengagement with the market economy. As an established independent curator and arts manager, Rann saw her role as acting as an unpaid representative and spokesperson, with a mandate to provide media and public information. No Lab resources were put toward associations with writers or publications, although several artists initiated writing collaborations to accompany exhibitions.[6]

Today, the Lab's philosophy can only be intuited from the traces of exhibitions and publications, from the website and the participants themselves. Never agreeing upon (and consequently not being held accountable to) a statement of intent, the Lab clearly knew what they were *not*. They set themselves in opposition to being solely a gallery, and particularly in opposition to ARI models that charge rental or hire fees. Otherwise, there was a reluctance to define or constrain a Lab identity. According to Rizkalla:

> We were constantly having dinners, with the intention of discussing what direction we should go in, how we were different from other spaces, but we never actually articulated it. There were always reasons for making a cohesive statement, but it didn't resolve the conflict. There was no manifesto, but we resolved certain things.

Tom Nicholson recalled being one of a number of people resistant to codifying the group's position over numerous conversations and heated arguments that frequently failed to find consensus. Rizkalla also stood firm against attempts to establish an organisational structure:

> We had lots of discussions about being a headless organisation, partly through my own personal neurosis, because inevitably people put Julie and myself at the helm, but we wouldn't have done it without this circle of friends. Otherwise, it would be completely different, a committee process.

An essential character of the Lab was its congenial hospitality, a value that created an environment for engaged conversation, and symbolised its ideology. Sociability helped to weave the sense of community that attracted the members. John Abbate was 'impressed with the idea of a group of people dedicated to experimental, research-based aesthetic practice and conversation. The Lab offered a way to keep a high-level conversation going outside the institutional context with a group of like-minded artists.' Similarly, Sandra Bridie found it significant to be part of a group with broad but shared interests. The group conversations also offered informal forms of exchange and support for Tom Nicholson. The cross-generational membership (which had precedents in other ARIs, including Store 5 in Melbourne), coupled with the artists' wide range of concerns and formal preoccupations, offered Raafat Ishak 'a way to explore and understand divergent practices, to set up and nurture friendships and share ordinary concerns, while contextualising my own practice and understanding of art making'. The Lab members formed a community of respect and a collective studio for dialogue that embraced existing colleagues and produced new national and international associations. Katherine Huang appreciated the occasions the Lab generated for extending critique and discussion: 'I became a member of a collective that was mutually supportive and interested in the artistic culture of Melbourne, as well as international practices. The Lab offered me a creative scope that incorporated and extended my own practice.'

Ocular Lab Inc. opened with the group project *Labrador* in October 2003. During the following year, the Lab had sixteen exhibitions that included solo exhibitions by members Loughrey, Sachs, Rizkalla, Mannall, Bridie and Louise Paramor, plus other visiting artists participating in collaborations or group exhibitions. The corner shop front space, which had been given a 'white cube' makeover, was assigned to members for an equal period each year (generally one month), in correlation with the flat organisational structure. The collegial environment is evident in the low attrition rate of members over the six years of the Lab, which was also facilitated by the ability to take periods of leave. On a member's departure, replacements were also recruited through existing networks. New members may not have enjoyed the same sense of cohesion as the original participants: 'We realised it was very difficult for someone to come into a group that has been running for a long time and which has its own dynamics, unless you have the time and energy to immerse yourself with in-depth involvement.'[7] However, the inclusiveness of the Lab was evident to Louise Paramor and Elvis Richardson, two artists who found a place at the Lab after living in other cities.

OPEN DOOR

> I liked the idea of 'curating a space of time', without censorship or the say-so of others in the group.
> —Sandra Bridie

By handing control of the space over to members during their allocated periods, the Lab's exhibition or event programming enjoyed a level of spontaneity. Each member could host any number of artists of their choice to work or exhibit in the space during their allotted term. Member Damiano Bertoli appreciated the autonomy that the equilateral management offered him and his invited exhibitors:

> Artists invited to participate or exhibit at Ocular Lab are able to construct a critical (or other) framework according to ideas generated from their practice, and shape the public outcomes of their work without depending on commercial, curatorial, and institutional influence. In this context, the artist is responsible for all decisions and outcomes.

Sally Mannall considered the capacity to extend use of the space to others as an exceptional opportunity for members to be closely involved in the realisation of their guests' projects and to mentor less-established artists. This perception of individual self-determination contributed to Rann's understanding of Lab members as a coherent intellectual and artistic group.

A fulsome schedule of exhibitions changing every two or three weeks, particularly during 2005–2007, is evidence that members took the opportunity to offer the space to known users and unscheduled guests during their allocated months. A scheduled winter recess of four to six weeks inserted further flexibility into the Lab's scheduling. It provided an additional elasticity that facilitated other exhibition possibilities or the use of the space as a studio, which often expedited preparation of a significant work or a collective project, not necessarily for exhibition at the Lab.

Although operating during a period when ARIs could access national and state funding (largely enabled over past decades by ARI lobbying), Ocular Lab remained staunchly independent from a state- or city-funded model. Rizkalla outlined the self-determination inherent in the collective's politics and philosophy:

> We didn't want to have to answer to others' priorities. We decided we could fund it ourselves. In the first year, everyone who had a show forked out the one hundred dollars a week, until the first fundraiser earned some cash. Only in that first year did exhibitors pay a fee. After that, the members covered the cost, and Lab members paid for their guests. It was based on simple mathematics: twelve artists, each responsible for one month's rent and costs. If anyone was tight, they shared the cost with the friends they curated in.

A small building and a good relationship with its lessor assisted in this autonomy, which did not exclude artists from bringing funding they had attracted to their own projects. Members eliminated any financial risk and the need for rental charges by dividing the annual fixed costs amongst themselves. The latter 'liberates the artist financially and enables further focus on the project and its realisation', as Damiano Bertoli noted, and extricated the Lab from compromising artists:

It is not easy for artist-run spaces to survive, so I would not want to be too moralistic about it, but the constraints — and the implicit contract between the space, the artist, and the work — which are established by the rental show negatively affect what can take place in an artist-run space. There is also an injustice to be resisted: the artist working for months on a body of work, which they must then pay to give to the public.

— Tom Nicholson

The Lab also differentiated itself from the process of programming through open calls and committees undertaken by other ARIs. There were no calls for exhibition proposals, nor were unsolicited proposals considered. Instead, interested artists were encouraged to find a rapport with one or more Lab members as the first step to further dialogue with the group. Ishak recalled that approaches to members were mostly initiated at exhibition openings, which were 'a significant social event for interpersonal contact and action, a realisation and consummation of these relationships'. This dialogic process was instrumental in shaping the Lab's network and its perceived ideological cohesion, as the relationships with the broader art community were established in discussion, and in social or artistic interaction, as a foundation for exchange and praxis.

SOCIAL COMMUNION

Experimentation in practice and thinking in the spirit of a laboratory applied equally to the potential of social relations at the Lab as it did to exhibitions and activities. Ishak recalled that:

> Initially, there were very few close or intimate relationships between Lab members. People got to know each other better and were able to establish good professional and personal connections. That didn't necessarily happen as a group. There were many smaller interactions within the group.

Arguably, the most important or appreciated legacy of the Lab was the collective hosting of visiting artists or curators, and the Lab dinners to which they and guests were invited. Dinners were prepared and served by members to guests at long tables in the gallery space, often accompanied by a talk or performance. These meals manifested a hospitable collegiality. They created a convivial context in which to meet visiting practitioners, and locate and discuss shared interests. As Loughrey recounts:

> The dinners were important for the type of dialogue that was encouraged. It was good for all Lab artists to meet visiting artists and vice versa. There was a generous, spirited feel about the occasions. Personally, I am not one for networking, but the idea of like-minded people getting together for a meal seemed a good, communal way of exchanging ideas and thoughts.

Hosting a group dinner was conducive to discussion for Mannall as it fostered a sense of community between a broad range of artists and arts professionals; visiting artists found a ready-made audience and a network that connected them 'into a community of practice, dialogue and support with the potential for exchange — intellectual, artistic, professional'. The meals presented an enabling model of 'generosity and simplicity in hosting' that was an encouragement to Sandra Bridie, opening 'up the role of practice beyond exhibition into one of mentorship, collaboration and geniality'. The glowing recollections of dinners from members and guests confirm the important role these events played in involving others in the community-based nature of the Lab, and in simultaneously energising its values and purpose. For Nicholson, hosting prompted reflection on both the nature of individual practice and the experimental attitude of the Lab:

> The principles of hosting became a very central part of how I understood the Lab, and a large part of what I enjoyed about it. It was a way to give over to other artists. It was a way to express hospitality and generosity toward another artist, and, in this way, to articulate something fundamental about the tradition of being an artist.

DISCURSIVE PROGRAMMING

> This is not to say that the physical space of an ARI is not a room with white walls, but the *relation* to space is not that of the white cube model, where space is understood as neutral, abstract, autonomous and void.[8]

Conscious of overstressing the distinctiveness of the group's collective existence, today Lab members prefer to prioritise the group rather than the space. By contrast, the art made and seen in that space, and discussed by participants and viewers, subsequently formed a significant record and symbol of the Lab's activities and purpose in the minds of its visitors.

The exhibition program extended the perception of the Lab as a 'community of dialogue'.[9] The cross-pollination of generations and practices supported a wide range of art and networks of local and international connections. An affiliation with the Melbourne ARI CLUBSproject Inc. transpired, assisted by their foundation member Terri Bird, who had previously been a member of *h. Project*. Open Spatial Workshop (OSW), comprising Terri Bird, Bianca Hester, Natasha Johns-Messenger and Scott Mitchell, exhibited *active air* in the Lab in 2005. CLUBS responded to the Lab's invitation to use their space in April 2006 by inviting Lab members to each contribute a work that was deployed within their project. The Lab engaged with this group of colleagues in a number of offsite exhibitions, including *mMa* at CLUBSproject Inc. (2005), and it participated in the *west Brunswick Sculpture Triennial* organised by OSW in 2009. The international presence was skewed toward Europe, and included Heike Baranowsky, Katrin von Maltzahn, Jan Svenungsson, Călin Dan, Ti Parks, as well as Jenny Gillam and Eugene Hansen from New Zealand.

It is impossible to attempt to describe the Lab's six-year exhibition history here. Rann aptly observed: 'a politics in many of the members' projects, a knowing anti-aesthetic for some and evident in others' interest in critiques of systems of production, be they of capital, art or knowledge, by pointing to their fissures. Not political art but critically engaged with the condition of being outside.' Examples of such exhibitions included: the flag projects of Nicholson denoting boundaries of different forms of sovereignty (2004 and 2005); the conjunction of history and contemporary social issues in Ishak's *Apparition of a miserable acquaintance* (2005); the return of history and the repressed in Bernhard Sachs' *The Polish Game* (2004) and *Regime iconoclaste d'un frisson: Le cercle vicieux après Salo / Iconoclastic Regime of the Shudder: The Vicious Circle after Salo* (2005); and the critique of nationalism in Canadian Cathy Busby's *Righting the wrongs* (2008). Several exhibitions and projects evoked topical issues in distinct ways, including: *W is for walking stick, war and witness* by Rizkalla (2004); Kylie Wilkinson's *NATIONALISM: What are you talking about?* and Kalle Runeson's examination of national space programs in *Fictionalizing Philosophers Comfort Zone* (both 2006);

Sean Loughrey's interrogations of assumptions regarding the technological versus natural world (2003, 2005); and Jonathan Luker's low-tech explorations of human/technological interfaces (2006, 2008).

Some members took the opportunity to hold 'retrospectives' of early work (Mannall and Ishak), or visitors displayed work on subjects of recurring interest (Bonita Ely and Ronnie van Hout in 2009). The majority presented new work, much of it designed to play with the space or making architectural modifications for the purpose (for example, Susan Jacobs with *For every solution there is problem*, in 2007). Solo exhibitions included a wide range of work: John Abbate's conceptual photographic projects (2004, 2005, 2007); Julie Davies' photographic insights into the overlooked and unseen (2005, 2008); Louise Paramor's images addressing gender and desire (2004); the intimate focus of Sally Mannall's video and photography (2004, 2005); and Sandra Bridie's curatorial programming and collaborations (2004, 2007). Collaborative projects stretched the boundaries of accustomed ways of working. The occasional group exhibitions of predominantly non-member artists inserted different ideas and interests, such as the varied perspectives on abstraction in *Inverted Topology* by Justin Andrews, Danny Lacy, Kyle Jenkins and Masato Takasaka in 2007.

The Lab was not exclusive — several members enjoyed the support of commercial galleries, and most were included in exhibitions at other artist-run initiatives or university or public galleries during their tenure as members. The inclusiveness of the Lab program fostered an overview of a diversity of forms and ideas in contemporary art and culture. It also reinforced the possibility of finding ways to exist as an artist and have an independent practice. The Lab's engagement with local artists and their peers advanced the assertion of cosmopolitanism within the cultural mix of Melbourne.

SITUATED PRAXIS AS ETHOS

> Some of our ambitions to expand the art dialogue worked, but not in formal ways. The Lab broke away from only being about visual art. It could be more of an intellectual gymnastic space than objects on the wall.
> — Alex Rizkalla

The Lab's indeterminate vision, flat line structure, delegation to individuals, socially-based operations, and antagonistic debate underpinned activity based in collective and independent action. In addition, the Lab's professional and theoretical diversity, 'while adding opportunity for a rich cross-pollination of ideas, gave an incredible "on the ground" sense of continuities and disjunctions in art history, theory, socio-political situations, practice, etc. across time — a rare and invaluable gift', as Rann noted. Articulating the development of a self-awareness of positionality at the Lab, Nicholson stated:

> This process — and specifically the de-centralised nature of the hosting mechanism — was how our 'doing' became our position. It made the idea of a statement redundant, or at least too reductive. The shows and practices that were generated by the Lab constituted its 'position'. The critical thing about this was that it was decentralised, that it was not about the policy statement of the group being followed in what was shown, but that the process of hosting articulated a position through forms and processes, through the language of artists.

Located in Brunswick, historically a working-class suburb of inner Melbourne, the Lab reflected the socio-economic situation of many Melbourne artists. Although it held a molecular position within an international artists' network, the Lab's location meant that it was invisible to that large section of the gallery-going public who were not interested in artists' and arts workers' close networks. An ex-milk bar situated at the crossroads of Pearson and Albert streets in Brunswick is democratic in concept, but, like most ARIs, for whom the general public is not a core constituency, the Lab only took small steps toward breaking down the boundaries of access.

The intentions articulated by Rizkalla on the occasion of the inaugural group project *Labrador* in late 2003 remained relevant throughout the six years of Lab operations:

> Our idea at present is a small collective of artists each with a two-month experimental project and responsibility of the space. This could be curatorial or structured around their work. The intention being that Ocular Lab is a laboratory where research and works in progress can be explored, to be shown later elsewhere to a wider audience and more public location.[10]

Members including Abbate agreed that the organic devolution of the exhibition calendar and lack of pressure to rent or open the space meant uncompromising but eclectic programming that possibly also contributed to a perception of exclusivity. In addition, as Nicholson noted, the interactions of artists across generations, practices and interests meant that this method of programming: 'emphasised people developing a relationship to the space and to the events and exchanges around the space before they showed there. The program reflected a certain attitude about art making. It was not conceived as being a space for everyone.' Selectivity was preferred to the popularism that stood for 'democracy' in institutions, according to Sachs:

> Rather, the concept of 'democracy' itself and the interrogation of mass opinions were among the objects of its scrutiny. Or at least potentially. The reality was somewhat different, but then again the history and measure of actuality is its manifest compendium of failure to live up to its ideals. And so it is with art and the Lab, which gives to the former and gave to the latter its urgency and its anarchic energy.

Off-site projects, such as *Labrador #2*, part of *2004: Australian Culture Now* at the Australian Centre for the Moving Image (2004), were possibilities for diversifying the audience while extending members' practices. However, these external projects were few in number. *Trinity Nine* at Trinity College, University of Melbourne (2004) was an opportunity taken by some members to test working in a site-specific situation.[11] The Lab required that any public project was to have a collective meaning or encourage exchange. Rann recalled making several suggestions for off-site projects that did not meet with a response, apart from the *Ocular Lab@Spacement* exhibition (19 April – 7 May 2005) that she curated with assistance from Rizkalla.

This indifference to public visibility, audience access and media coverage signalled the Lab's concentration on the exploration of practice within its own space. Rizkalla described the Lab as being closest to the notion of a laboratory when projects were created *in situ* without constraints such as time pressures. An example was Ian Whittlesea's evolving painting project (2009). Research interests were facilitated by the library of arts writer Robert Schubert, held at the Lab on loan. Loughrey noted the lack of concessions to audiences: 'The Lab offered audiences a diverse number of shows. Whether they were politically, conceptually or socially difficult, most shows had a tough, experimental proposition.' Similarly, Ishak saw members sharing expectations of a peer audience:

> What the Lab offered visitors was a way to rethink and renegotiate the way artists work. It was an opportunity for artists to experiment, produce work that had a slightly obscure or private meaning — in a sense, it was like a drawing or sketching space. Most artists knew that responses to their work would be educated or knowledgeable responses.

ARI: ARTISTS RESOLUTELY INDEPENDENT

Reflecting on recent projects at the Victorian College of the Arts Margaret Lawrence Gallery, director Vikki McInnes made a case for the importance of 'dialogue, with practice, with ideas and with each other' and appealed for more dialogic conversations to be manifest in public.[12] Her appeal highlights the loss of knowledge that occurs when thinking archivally. Discussion, such as the discursive collegiality that is the history of the Lab, exists only in private, recorded in the minds of the members and the productive connections made between works or individuals. This is the virtual narrative that Lev Manovich suggests the material database fails to embrace.[13]

From their perspective, members find a range of various evident and implicit legacies remaining from Ocular Lab:

> I think the legacy of artists' spaces is a collective legacy that keeps on growing with the emergence of new spaces. The sum of all spaces offers a wide range of possibilities. In a way, I don't think any one space is complete in its achievement; there always something missing and it could very well be the next space that comes up.
>
> Having said that, if there is one thing that the Lab achieved that I think is exemplary, it is the way we managed to create something that was useful, sometimes contentious, and slightly academic in its pursuits, which remained inherently unambitious. Artist-run spaces can sometimes operate like stepping stones for other things. I think the Lab tried to do the opposite. In a way, what each artist did was take a risk, sometimes as an antithesis to his or her own practice. We managed to get away with it because we were each confident in our own practice and basically had a life outside the Lab.
>
> — Raafat Ishak

Katherine Huang perceived the Lab as being neither unique nor finished, residing in an 'idea of an open model for an artist-run space that is not application-based, that emphasised dialogue, collaborative as well as individual outputs ... unconstrained by unbending funding imperatives or programming timelines'. One member is pursuing a subsequent independent initiative to involve other networks.[14] In the larger picture, Rann situated the Lab in a national history alongside 'the conceptually underpinned and/or collective models started by Inhibodress (1970–72) in Sydney, Art Projects (1979–84), Store 5 (circa 1989–93) and Basement Gallery (1994–96) in Melbourne — for the purpose of exhibition, experimentation and dialogue with peers.'

The features that differentiated the Lab — autonomy from funding and the market, collegiality and networks, the program — laid the genesis of its particular consequences: a model of hospitality, an exchange and support network that offered a context and sustained a sense of community driven by art and artists, and significant audience experiences. The Lab's 'family ties' of networks, dinners, discussions and exhibitions brought together art, ideas, bodies, propositions, movements and experiences in a collective play, a frisson of debate and private discussion. The gift Ocular Lab leaves is the inspiration for productive individual and collective dialogue as essential to art making. The Lab's short history is in one feature reminiscent of the mapping of the human genome: the finding of new knowledge by the simultaneous negotiation of multiple, networked and unresolved paths, undertaken by individuals refusing to bend to unanimity or compromise.

1 Comments by Ocular Lab members are from email correspondence during June and July 2010 and are separately credited only when derived from a different source.

2 See Jones, B. 'Why artist-run space?' in Heagney, D. ed., 2007, *Making Space: Artist-run initiatives in Victoria*, Melbourne: VIA-N, p. 18. This publication provides a useful overview of recent artist-run initiatives in Victoria and the context of their development.

3 Davies and Rizkalla had cemented numerous connections during a 1995–96 residency in Berlin.

4 The Lab demonstrated many characteristics generally associated with ARIs: a small-scale exhibition space, initiated and patronised by artists with studios in proximity, avoidance of a house style by the mix of members, yet development of a group signature. A forerunner of the Lab's approach to the space as a site of work and production in Melbourne was Art Projects (1979–84), in which John Nixon had eliminated the barriers between studio and display space. The ARI as a facilitator of international and interstate networks and exchange similarly had a history in Melbourne, for example in the overseas connections made by West Space and the association between 1st Floor and CBD in Sydney in the latter 1990s.

5 This was apparent in Sachs' 2004 project at Ocular Lab, *(Reconstruction of) The Polish Game*.

6 The association of artists and writers characterised Fitzroy's 1st Floor when it commenced in 1993. According to Kirsten Rann, the Lab discussed the partnering of artists and writers, and several artists invited writers to participate, including Justin Clemens for *Performance Anxiety*, curated by Damiano Bertoli, and Stephen Zagala for *The Decadence of the Nude*, curated by Raafat Ishak (both in 2004). Clemens also wrote for Bertoli's solo exhibition *Continuous Moment: Hot August Knife* (2005). Email from Kirsten Rann to the author, 12 August 2010.

7 Interview with Julie Davies, 3 July 2010. John Abbate, Louise Paramor, Bernhard Sachs and Kirsten Rann resigned at different times from Ocular Lab and Katherine Huang, Jonathan Luker and Elvis Richardson were incoming members.

8 Attiwill, S. 'Spatial Relations' in Heagney, op.cit., p. 32.

9 An outline of the program is archived at http://www.ocularlabinc.com/index_09calander.html. Programming included a small exterior 'billboard' project during 2007–2009, showing three to four works each year.

10 Rizkalla in Crawford, A. 'In the eye of the beholder', *The Age*, A3, Thursday 6 November 2003, p. 9.

11 *Trinity Nine* at Trinity College at the University of Melbourne consisted of work by Abbate, Bridie, Davies, Ishak, Loughrey, Mannall, Nicholson and Rizkalla, and texts by Melbourne writers and curators responding to situations in and around the college.

12 McInnes, V., 'Bureau' in Daw, K. & V. McInnes eds., 2008, *Bureau*, Melbourne: Margaret Lawrence Gallery, p. 10.

13 Manovich, L., 2001, *The Language of New Media*, Roger Malina ed., Leonardo, Cambridge, London: MIT Press, p. 231.

14 Director Brett Jones indicated the priority and importance of ARI West Space in 1998 as: 'it's the sense of community, the sense of place, the engagement of ideas and sustained work, which doesn't happen in a lot of other places for artists'. Jones, B. 'Interview with Brett Jones, West Space Inc. October 1997' in Bridie, S., (co-ordinator), 1998, *Artists/Artist-Run Spaces: Interviews with artists from six Melbourne artists' spaces*, Melbourne: Talk Artists Initiative and West Space, p. 4. In contrast to Ocular Lab, West Space had at the time established an intention to play an instrumental role in the contemporary art sector, by providing forums and publications for artists and audiences and seeking ways to gain institutional benefits or recognition for the independent artist-led organisation.

PERFORMANCE ANXIETY

Justin Clemens

So, you've got performance anxiety. Everyone knows you can do it; you know you can do it. You're talented. You went to art school. You've had successes. But, somehow, it hasn't quite worked. You're not quite where you thought you'd be. You get nervous, go all weird, don't talk to the right people, don't talk in the right way, don't quite make the work that people are going crazy for right now, and then, whenever you think about it, you go a bit funny, get even weirder. You can't perform. But what's stopping you? Don't you think you're good enough? Maybe you're not, but you can't seem to give it up, either. So why not just relax? It'll be OK. In fact, it'll be better than if you worry too much. People will appreciate your efforts; they may even think you're hot, love you even. You may even enter art history, may even be considered an important artist. People will write elegant and witty catalogue essays about your work. But, still, knowing this, you worry too much. Sweating, trembling, stuttering, paralysed, all sorts of embarrassing physical reactions, way in excess of any possible conscious control. And so it all fucks up. Or, at least, that's how you feel. How could you do it, keep doing it, again and again? Do you like the humiliation? The frustration? The physical horror of it? What is it that you want? But that's it, isn't it? It's your desire: bigger, nastier, more inadmissible even than your (not-so) secret ambitions to dominate the world, be the best, most famous, best-loved, richest artist in existence. Anyone can have those ambitions; actually, probably everyone does have those ambitions. Even people who aren't artists. The problem is, you are an artist, maybe even a real artist, and so you don't, can't, have a clue what you want, other than that it's so obscene and extraordinary there aren't any words, images, objects up to the job. And so, when you try to start making, the catastrophe of nothingness erupts, vitiating the work from within. But without that nothingness, without the anxiety that accompanies it, without the irreparable and unbearable sense of impending failure hovering over the whole affair, it wouldn't feel worth it, and it wouldn't be. Catastrophic as performance anxiety can be, things would be worse without it.

ARCHITECTONIC TRACES

Melanie Irwin

Sandie Bridie invited me to undertake a two-week residency at Ocular Lab in April 2008. The residency gave me the opportunity to spread my materials out in a space that was approximately six times the size of the studio that I had at the time at the Victorian College of the Arts. I live in West Brunswick and it was valuable for me to have access to the space, which was walking distance from my house. I generated a large-scale, wall-based installation work using tree branches that I had found in public spaces around Brunswick. The weekend before my residency, there'd been violent, windy storms, so it was easy to find branches that had fallen down, near Jewell Station and in Temple Park. I nailed the branches into the walls vertically so that their shapes jutted out against a hot-pink geometric wall-drawing, and then I wound cotton thread around the branches horizontally, from one end of the work to the other. I was interested in approaching the architecture in a morphological manner, and I thought of the thread as tracing the action of my body through the space, so I titled the work *Architectonic traces*. I also tested some other, smaller-scale experiments alongside the installation, using leftover branches and twigs and the vice that I'd been using to grip the branches as I sawed through them. For another piece, I used white chalk and a ruler to map the trajectory of a ball of cotton thread that repeatedly spun and rolled across the floor as I measured lengths of the thread against my arm span. The results of these tests still inform my methodology. The residency culminated in a one-day exhibition, where I met other Lab members, and friends from the neighbourhood came along to see the outcomes of my investigations.

A DEVELOPING RELATIONSHIP

Katrin von Maltzahn and Jan Svenungsson

Since first meeting Julie Davies and Alex Rizkalla in 1995 at Künstlerhaus Bethanien in Berlin, we have seen our relationship with Australia and Australian culture develop.

We both made our first visits to Melbourne, although not together, in 1998 for exhibitions at the *h. Project*, which Julie and Alex instigated. The space that would later become Ocular Lab was then Alex's crowded studio. Katrin remembers Julie saying something about the possibility of making exhibitions there, at some later date.

In the meantime, we got to know Tom Nicholson, who arrived in Berlin in 2001 with Katrin's phone number given to him by Julie. Soon, all three of us were close friends, and this relationship led to *course*, Jan's first exhibition at Ocular Lab, with Tom, in 2005.

Jan couldn't travel to this exhibition, but we were able to return to Melbourne in 2007 for a joint residency at the RMIT School of Art. A couple of days after our arrival, we opened an exhibition at Ocular Lab together, called *Being the Mirror*. We were treated to an Ocular Lab dinner, and the generosity of the Lab group of friends and collaborators (many of whom, in different capacities, would invest themselves in helping make our six weeks in Melbourne superbly rewarding) made a deep impression on us.

Being two artists together, one thing we had always avoided is making joint exhibitions. This was our first. Both of us had chosen a group of work to exhibit: Katrin a large group of small drawings depicting components of a disassembled computer, and Jan five drawings in which he tries to work out a way to fuse two written languages into one. In our new-found spirit of exchange, we had then switched works between us and each one had developed a new work based on the other's work: a translation or a transformation.

It was an exciting process. How much will be retained of the original meaning, if you make the other's artwork into your own? Not as appropriation, but as dialogic material. How much information can *really* be exchanged between people... and cultures? These questions play out also in our own daily lives, as we do not share the same nationality. And when we come to Australia — even though we have made so many good friends there and feel 'at home' in many ways — there are always interesting aspects of cultural difference which will play out in subtle ways.

This experience of difference motivates us to return, as Jan did in 2010. His purpose then was focused around a visit to Papunya, a name known precisely because of cultural translation.

OCULAR LAB / SOUTH PROJECT

Magdalena Moreno

South and Ocular Lab have always shared a common language: a clear and simple purpose of openness and deep respect based around people; valuing coming together and sharing; and a sense of documentation and access, to extend experiences beyond those lucky to be present.

For these, and many and varied other reasons, South and Ocular Lab found themselves working together on numerous occasions. Interestingly, no contracts, no MOUs, no formal money exchanges, no paper trail. However, there was a deep understanding of *why*, and so the *how* always somehow fell into place. The Lab/South Dinners became iconic. With visiting artists from as near as other suburbs and as far away as São Paulo, Porto Alegre, Johannesburg, Santiago, Auckland and many other places in the south, we came together for a meal, for a yarn, and to find that our language of the arts, creative expression and profound investigation was a *lingua franca*.

The infused scent of the meals was the welcome, the long, white table was an invitation to participate that did not expect you to be anything other than yourself and, well, the rest was an experience that has led to so many collaborations. Try to formalise, categorise, curate, affect, and manage a space like this... well, it simply would not work. That's what was so special about these dinners.

As South grew over the years and developed a range of international projects, the relationship with Ocular Lab was always present.

As the Lab reflects on its years of activation, so does the South Project. How fitting that both are resulting in a publication...

I have a strong belief, though, that such projects/ideas are like incubators. They bring people together, and provide a safe and creative space for dialogue. Maybe the Lab and South have fulfilled their purposes, and now it rests on those who participated to take those values and create their own forms.

TRINITY NINE

Jane O'Neill

There were two distinct audiences for the exhibition initiated by Ocular Lab at Trinity College, at the University of Melbourne, in 2007. There were people who experienced the work incidentally as part of their everyday surroundings, and others who visited the college specifically to see the exhibition. In various ways, the exhibition revealed much about the inherent habits of the occupants and the designs of the surrounding buildings.

Flanked by a green oval, a solid church and creeping ivy along stone walls, Trinity College is the oldest residential college on campus. As with many of the colleges at the University of Melbourne, it is a mixture of Victorian charm and more recent architectural additions. Sean Loughery depended upon the co-operation of students for his fluorescent pink geometric installation in the windows of the dormitories of the 1965 Cowan Building. In the photographic documentation, the work forms two triangles in a way that suggests an extension of space which reaches beyond the rooftops into the sky. On the day I visited, there were signs that students had neglected their role in the collaboration; debris was littered in front of the screens, and, in some cases, the screens were entirely absent. What remained was a poignant demonstration of the futility often involved in aesthetic collaboration. Just near the Cowan Building, Raafat Ishak's large black box was perched in a tree — a sculptural headquarters of sorts. With connotations of safety and surveillance, the box provided a focal point and link for the works exhibited throughout the campus. In the lower arcade of the Evan Burge building, Julie Davies transformed the columns with vertical photographs of rat paws in such a way that they resembled the repetitive patterned configurations of breeze blocks from the sixties.

For the Ocular Lab artists, the library was a ripe backdrop for the introduction of different methods of categorisation. John Abbate chose to re-order books according to colour and texture, whilst Sandra Bridie submitted Ocular Lab's own library of books for perusal throughout the duration of the exhibition. Tom Nicholson isolated the books from the Marxist writings section to a more visible area in the library and filled the space left behind with a video projection of his Trades Hall project. Along the sides of the bookshelves, Raafat Ishak installed small portraits of childhood friends. In this context, Ishak's paintings prompted rumination about the ways we order and filter various phases of life. There was warmth to Alex Rizkalla's curiosity cabinets, inspired by Samuel Beckett's *Endgame*. These collages of collected objects existed in stark contrast to the otherwise standardised surfaces of filing cabinets and laminated desks. By the time I saw Sally Mannall's film, it was also screened in the library (on the opening night, it was projected onto the back wall of the squash court). Mannall's recording of rowers training in confined pools of grimy water speaks most arrestingly of the Sisyphean battles of everyday life. Finally, I ventured (with permission) into the dining hall. The students were having lunch, but Damiano Bertoli's dislocated individuals fitted beautifully with the experience of viewing the work. At every step of the way, I felt as though nudged, gently, to question the accepted means of order and categorisation in this environment.

OCULAR LAB

Ian Whittlesea

Something I often have in mind is Robert Barry's text piece that says:

> A place to which we can come, and for a while, be free to think about what we are going to do. — Marcuse

It's as good a description of Ocular Lab as any.

The thing I made there was unlike my work before or since, but perhaps that is the point (or one of the points) of going somewhere else for a while. Being a long way from home allows a level of re-invention, as well as a more prosaic distance from the daily humdrum that normally circumscribes what we make and how we think about it.

Or, to put it another way, at the Lab I felt free to think and do exactly what I wished without wondering (or caring) what others might make of it.

At some point in each residency, there is a dinner in the gallery, where the resident speaks about their work to the members of the Lab. I was rather dreading the dinner. As I prepared my Powerpoint, it felt like I was being made to sing for my supper. Almost as an afterthought, I included a few images of an ongoing (and perpetually unfinished) project, the translation of Yves Klein's book *Les Fondements de Judo* into English.

Of course, the dinner was wonderful, the wine and conversation flowed, and when I stood up to speak about my work, it no longer felt like an obligation, but a chance to say 'thank you' — to Sandra Bridie for her support over many years, to my hosts Greg and Sally (who put up with me sleeping in their spare room and drinking their Cointreau for a month) and to Rubie for introducing me to *She's the Man*.

The talk about my work seemed to go well, but what was interesting was the reaction to my final few slides. People were genuinely enthusiastic about the judo project, in a way that I'd not expected. I'd worked on the book for so long that I'd lost sight of the fact that people might actually want to see and talk about it. The experience gave me the energy to come back to London and lock myself away for a month until the work on the book was finished.

In the end, it wasn't the solitude or the chance to make new work that was of most value, it was the honest and spontaneous reactions of other artists.

So, once again, thank you Ocular Lab for a project of love and generosity.

CHRONOLOGY

2003

OCTOBER
Labrador, John Abbate, Damiano Bertoli, Julie Davies, Raafat Ishak, Sean Loughrey, Sally Mannall, Louise Paramor, Alex Rizkalla, Bernhard Sachs and Chris Ulbrick.

NOVEMBER
Natural Selections, Sean Loughrey.

DECEMBER
Gom.Brick, Shane Moore.

2004

FEBRUARY
La Kinky Beat, David Jolly and David Franzke.

MARCH
Performance Anxiety, Fiona Abicare, Christian Capurro, Andrew Hurle, Eliza Hutchison, Tom Nicholson and Rose Nolan; curated by Damiano Bertoli.
Decadence of the Nude, Karen Burns, Raafat Ishak, Jonathan Nichols, Sangeeta Sandrasegar, Vivienne Shark LeWitt, Lara Travis and Stephen Zagala; curated by Jonathan Nichols and Raafat Ishak.

APRIL
Valentine's Manifesto to Lust, Deborah Gardner.
Madchen Club and 'Other Stuff', Louise Paramor.
DeliCATE Pop-ecology 3, Geoff Overheu.

MAY
TRIAGE, John Abbate, Naomi Williamson and Andrew Frost.

JUNE
The Polish Game, Bernhard Sachs.

OCTOBER
Momento Horribilis: W is for walking stick, war and witness, Alex Rizkalla.

NOVEMBER
Lapse, Sally Mannall.
The Fitting, Claire Lambe.

DECEMBER
Ocular Lab Fundraiser.
Signals, Jonathan Luker.
The Doppler Effect (Part 1), Sandra Bridie, Ruth Claxton (UK), Felicity Greenland and Kelly Large (UK).
Wait, Sandra Bridie and Cynthia Troup.

2005

FEBRUARY
A Study of the Insignificant, Julie Davies.
Autopilot, Greg Richards.

MARCH
Active Air, Open Spatial Workshop.
Doppler Effect #2, Ruth Claxton (UK) and Kelly Large (UK).

APRIL
Roarers, Kit Wise.
Speed Space, Sean Loughrey.

MAY
Continuous Moment: Hot August Knife, Damiano Bertoli.

JUNE
Disassembling, Sally Mannall.
Hoddle Street Massacre, Elvis Richardson.

JULY
Course, Tom Nicholson and Jan Svenungsson (Sweden).
Photo-graph, John Abbate.

AUGUST
Situations, Richard Lewer, John Abbate and Vin Ryan.

SEPTEMBER
Apparition of a miserable acquaintance, Raafat Ishak.
Central Core Component from Centre of the Universe, Hany Armanious.

OCTOBER
Regime iconoclaste d'un frisson: le cercle vicieux après Salo Iconoclastic (*Regime of the Shudder: the Vicious Circle after Salo*), Bernhard Sachs.

NOVEMBER
4HZ, Simon Terrill.
Early Fabricated, curated by Salvatore Panatteri.

2006

JANUARY
Flag Time: Marat at his Last Breath, Tom Nicholson.

MARCH
NATIONALISM: What are you talking about?, Kylie Wilkinson.
Out of the Blue, Heike Baranowsky (Germany); curated by Liza Vasiliou.

APRIL
Clubs@Ocular Lab.

MAY
The Pro(d)a(u)ct of Love, Utako Shindo, curated by Kirsten Rann.
White Cube, Nick Devlin and Monique De Ponsardin; curated by Kirsten Rann.
Assemblages and Drawings, Katherine Huang.

JUNE
My Blue Heaven, Mark McDean.

AUGUST
Wood Nymph Triptych (the heart is a lonely hunter), Neil Emmerson.
Fictionalising Philosophers Comfort Zone, Kalle Runeson (Sweden).

SEPTEMBER
No, Alex Rizkalla.
Fan Flag Six, Sean Loughrey and Raafat Ishak.

OCTOBER
Hung Out to Dry, Nick Selenitsch.
Console Network, Jonathan Luker.

NOVEMBER
New Work, Julia Gorman, Estelle Ihasz, Rossana Martinez, Masato Takasaka, Toby Paterson, John Nixon and Charles Wilton; curated by Danny Lacy.

2007

JANUARY
Inverted Topology, Justin Andrews, Danny Lacy, Kyle Jenkins and Masato Takasaka.
Billboard, Sean Loughrey.

FEBRUARY
Being the Mirror, Katrin Von Maltzahn (Germany) and Jan Svenungsson (Sweden).

MARCH
Documents from a banner marching project 2004–2007, Tom Nicholson.
Manifesto Drawing: Representatives, Greg Creek.

APRIL
Victoria Victoria!, Sarah Goffman.
'Transcultural mutations & the importance of the prefix Meta-', Ocular Lab artists.
Billboard: Andrew McQualter.

MAY
Ocular Lab Retrospective Project #1: Sandra Bridie.
One-month residency: Mia Salsjo.

JUNE
The Unprecedented Dark Light of the New Letters, Elizabeth Newman.
I Like My Old Stuff Better Than Your New Stuff (More prog rock sculptures from the 5th dimension), Masato Takasaka.

AUGUST
Objects and projections, John Abbate.
It's a Lovely Daze, Jenny Gillam and Eugene Hansen.

SEPTEMBER
R is for relics, remains and ruins, Alex Rizkalla and Victor Georgopoulos.

OCTOBER
Lane Cormick and Tony Garifalakis.
For every Solution there is a Problem, Susan Jacobs.
Billboard: Peter Tyndall.

NOVEMBER
New Diagonal, Laresa Kosloff.
Moya McKenna and Brad Westmoreland.

DECEMBER
Ocular retrospective project #2: Raafat Ishak.

2008

FEBRUARY
Composite Portraits of Sandra Bridie, Julie Davies and Sandra Bridie.

MARCH
The Garden of Eden, Zoe Ali and Christos Tsiolkas.
Site Projects, Sean Loughrey and William Seeto.

MAY
GENERA, Fiona Macdonald.

JULY
Righting the Wrongs, Cathy Busby (Canada).

AUGUST
Ocular Lab Fundraiser

SEPTEMBER
Wallets etc. and *A Selection from the 10,000 Collages*, Ti Parks (UK).
Ocular Lab Retrospective project #3: Sally Mannall.

OCTOBER
Magnolia Caboose Babyfinger, Ry Haskings.

NOVEMBER
Asynchronous, Jonathan Luker.
Collaboration, Jonathan Luker and Alex Rizkalla.
New Work, Darryl Cordell, David Franzke and Victoria Huf.

DECEMBER
A SLOW FADE. TO BLACK, Ian Whittlesea (UK).

2009

FEBRUARY
The Collection Show, Sandra Bridie, Damiano Bertoli, Julie Davies and Alex Rizkalla, Raafat Ishak, Sean Loughrey, Sally Mannall, Tom Nicholson, Elvis Richardson.
Fallenness, Ronnie Van Hout.

APRIL
Let's Get Boweried, Nat Thomas and Consertina Inserra, part of *Get Oak Firmness*, curated by Elvis Richardson, Hell Gallery.
Renny Kodgers 'The Model', Mark Shorter, part of *Get Oak Firmness*, curated by Elvis Richardson.

MAY
Ultra Primo, Claire Lambe, part of *Get Oak Firmness*, curated by Elvis Richardson.
Billboard: Cameron Robbins.

JUNE
Emotional Architecture: Recent Developments, Călin Dan.

AUGUST
Greetings comrades, the image has now changed its status, Bridget Crone.
The Murray's Edge, Bonita Ely.
Billboard: Sally Mannall.

SEPTEMBER
Quinto Sesto; Fighting for Peace (1975–76), Institute of Contemporary Art Newtown.

OCTOBER
Open Residency Project, Lisa Kelly.
Billboard: Jonathan Luker.

NOVEMBER
Pissing in the Infinity Pool, Rob McLeish.
Liminal Work, Marcel Feillafe.
The Joy of Living, Kellie Wells.

DECEMBER
You're the Cunt, Donut, Kate Smith.

2010

FEBRUARY
The cabinet of unnatural history – souvenirs of the last century, Alex Rizkalla and Igor Listkiewicz.

OFF-SITE PROJECTS

2004

Labrador #2, a video project as part of *2004: Australian Culture Now* at ACMI/NGV.

2005

Ocular Lab: 12, curated by Kirsten Rann and Alex Rizkalla, at Spacement Gallery, Melbourne: John Abbate, Damiano Bertoli, Sandra Bridie, Julie Davies, Raafat Ishak, Sean Loughrey, Sally Mannall, Tom Nicholson, Louise Paramor, Alex Rizkalla and Bernhard Sachs.

2006

Trinity Nine, at Trinity College, The University of Melbourne: John Abbate, Damiano Bertoli, Sandra Bridie, Julie Davies, Raafat Ishak, Sean Loughrey, Sally Mannall, Tom Nicholson and Alex Rizkalla.

Ocular Lab – Pagework, editor: Sandra Bridie, Ocular Lab Inc, 2005. Contributions by John Abbate, Damiano Bertoli, Sandra Bridie, Julie Davies, Raafat Ishak, Sean Loughrey, Sally Mannall, Tom Nicholson, Kirsten Rann, Alex Rizkalla and Bernhard Sachs. Presented as a part of the exhibition *Active Imagination*, Birmingham, UK, 2006

2007

Ocular Notes, at George Paton Gallery, The University of Melbourne: John Abbate, Sandra Bridie, Julie Davies, Raafat Ishak, Sean Loughrey, Jonathan Luker, Sally Mannall, Elvis Richardson and Alex Rizkalla.

2009

Instruction Models, a collaborative project between Ocular Lab, CLUBSproject, and students from the Otago Polytechnic School of Art, at Blue Oyster Art Project Space, Dunedin, New Zealand.

The Gift, an exchange exhibition at the Institute of Contemporary Art Newtown, Sydney: Sandra Bridie, Damiano Bertoli, Raafat Ishak, Sean Loughrey, Jonathan Luker, Sally Mannall, Tom Nicholson and Elvis Richardson.

ACKNOWLEDGMENTS

Alex Pittendrigh, Alexie Glass-Kantor, Andrew Hurle, Andrew McQualter, Annie Wilson, Bianca Hester, Bill Seeto, Cameron Robbins, Carla Ceson, Catherine Clover, Christian Capurro, Claire Lambe, David Jolly, David Noonan, David Thomas, David Young, Deborah Garden, Eliza Hutchison, Fiona Abicare, Geoff Overheu, Greg Richards, Hany Armanious, Helen Johnson, Jane O'Neill, Jennifer Mills, Jess Johnson, Jon Cattapan, Jordan Marani, Justin Clemens, Kate Smith, Kit Wise, Laresa Kosloff, Laylah Ali, Lily Hibberd, Lisa Young, Elizabeth Newman, Magdalena Moreno, Mark Hislop, Mark McDean, Masato Takasaka, Matt Hinkley, Max Delany, Melanie Irwin, Merrin Eirth, Mira Gojek, Neil Emmerson, Nick Devlin, Nick Mangan, Nick Selenitch, Pat Foster & Jen Berean, Peter Grizwotz, Peter J. Burke, Peter Tyndall, Ricky Swallow, Ry Haskings, Sadie Chandler, Sangeeta Sandrasegar, Sarah Goffman, Scott Miles, Simon Terrill, Steig Persson, Susan Jacobs, Terri Bird, Ty Parks, Vikki McInnes, Zoe Ali, Gertrude Contemporary, Monash University Museum of Art, South Project.

Justin Clemens' essay 'Performance Anxiety' was originally written for the catalogue of the exhibition *Performance Anxiety*, 2004, curated by Damiano Bertoli.

Brad Haylock is a lecturer in the Faculty of Art, Design & Architecture, Monash University.

front and back covers:
Transcultural mutations & the importance of the prefix Meta- Sally Mannall, Greg Richardson and Alex Rizkalla working during the project, 2007.

inside front cover and page 1:
Raafat Ishak, Sean Loughrey and Tom Nicholson, installing *The Collection Show*, 2009.

page 2:
Damiano Bertoli and Raafat Ishak making the Ocular Lab sign, 2004.

page 115:
Hosting for Ocular Lab Retrospective Project #1: Sandra Bridie, 2007. Damiano Bertoli, Kirsten Rann, Alex Rizkalla, Lucas Ihlein, Sandra Bridie and Bernhard Sachs.

page 116 and inside back cover:
Alex Rizkalla and Victor Georgopoulos installing the project *R is for relics, remains and ruins*, 2007.

Hostings: Ocular Lab, 2003–2010

Editors: Julie Davies and Brad Haylock
Essays: Zara Stanhope and Stephen Zagala
Design: Brad Haylock
Proofreading: Simone Calderwood
Prepress & Printing: BPA Print Group
Typeset in Bau Pro

First edition 2012
ISBN: 978-1-922099-00-6

Published by Surpllus Pty Ltd

Ocular Lab Inc. has received generous financial assistance and support in producing this publication, from:
Mrs Vignouli and Vince Vignouli;
Moreland City Council through the Community Development Grants Program; and
VCA Margaret Lawrence Gallery.

Surpllus Pty Ltd
PO Box 418
Flinders Lane 8009
Victoria, Australia
www.surpllus.com

Surpllus #9

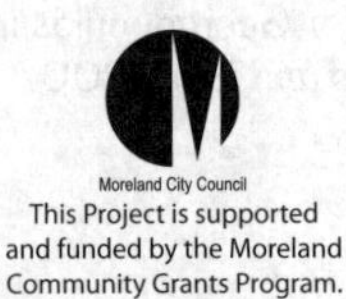

This Project is supported and funded by the Moreland Community Grants Program.

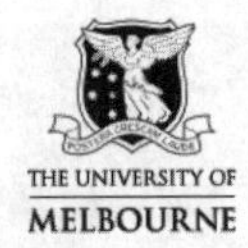

THE UNIVERSITY OF MELBOURNE

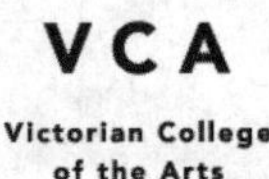

Victorian College of the Arts

ocular lab inc

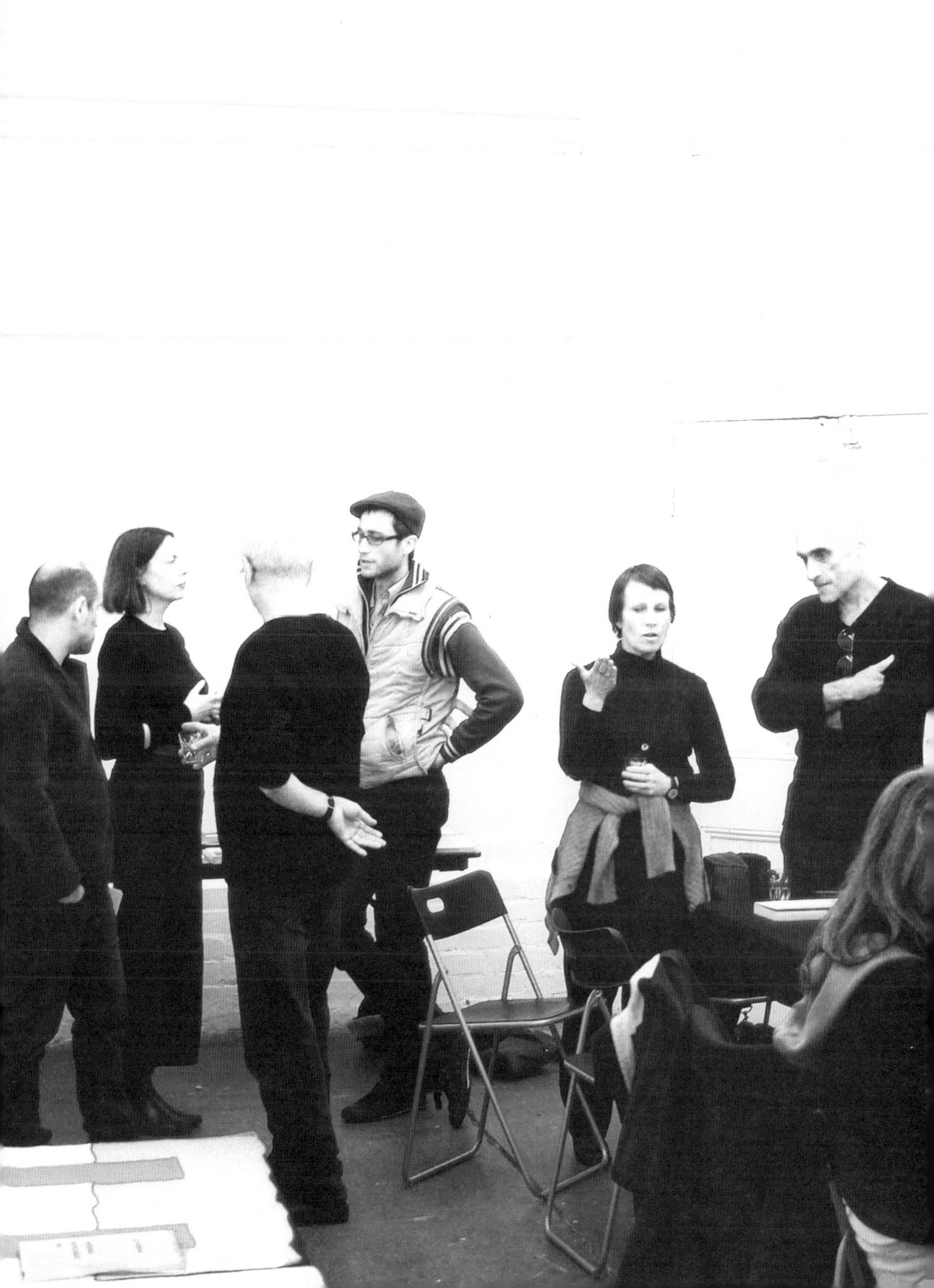

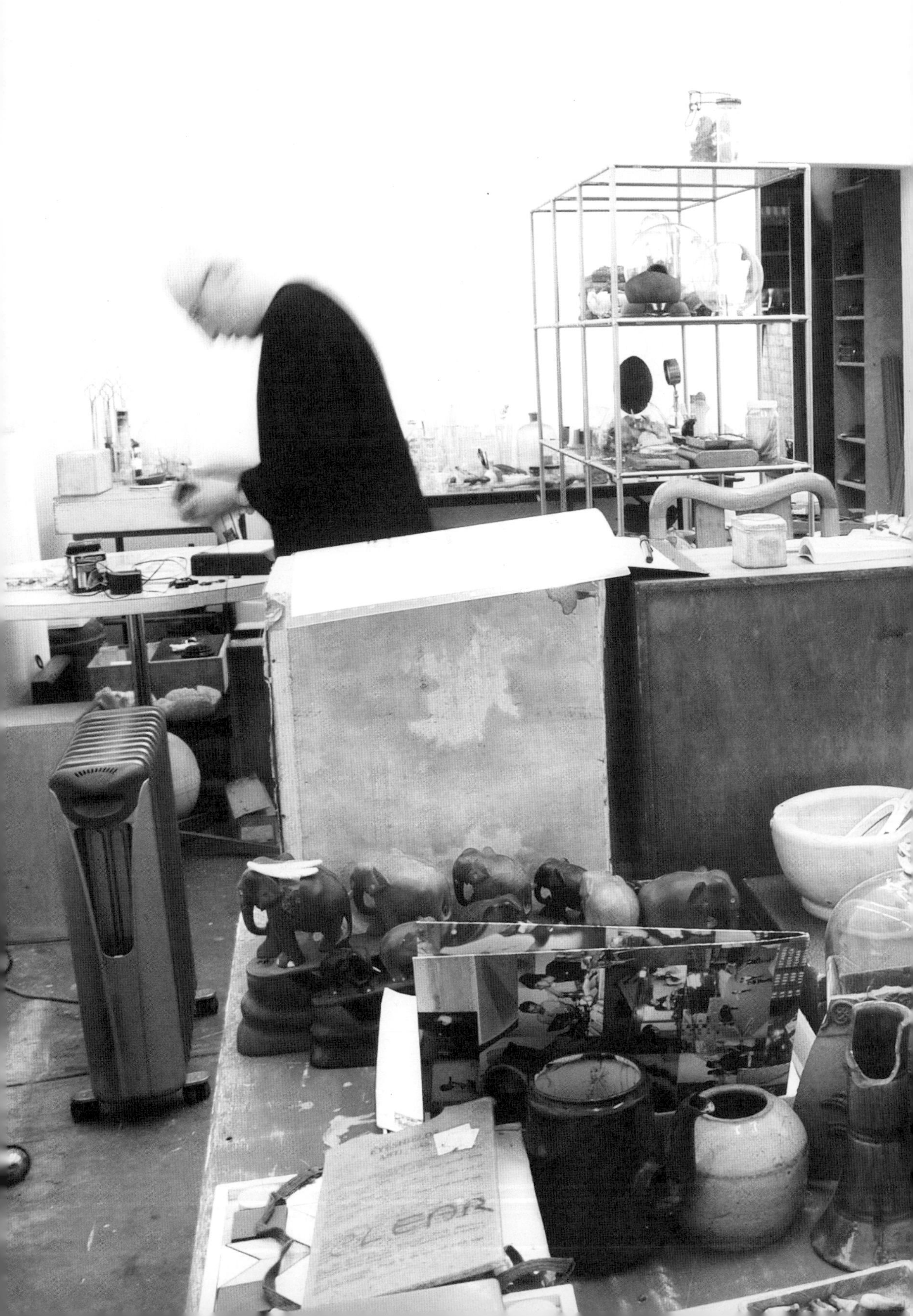
EAR